SWIFT

An Introduction

SWIFT

An Introduction

By

RICARDO QUINTANA

GEOFFREY CUMBERLEGE
OXFORD UNIVERSITY PRESS
LONDON   NEW YORK   TORONTO
1955

Oxford University Press, Amen House, London E.C.4

GLASGOW NEW YORK TORONTO MELBOURNE WELLINGTON
BOMBAY CALCUTTA MADRAS KARACHI CAPE TOWN IBADAN

Geoffrey Cumberlege, Publisher to the University

Printed in Great Britain by
The Camelot Press Ltd., London and Southampton

TO

J. M. Q.

PREFACE

I TRUST that the purpose of this short study of Swift will be sufficiently clear from my title and table of contents. No attempt has been made to treat of Swift's career in anything approaching full detail. My object has been, rather, to suggest the forms, the contours, which can now be discerned in his life and his achievement. What is discerned is a matter, of course, of who does the discerning. Occasionally, no doubt, I shall be found speaking for myself. It would be surprising if this were not so, since I have lived with Swift for a good many years and have arrived at certain views concerning both his art and various episodes in his personal life which must naturally colour many of the things I have to say. But though the personal element may perhaps be greater than I imagine, it is inconsiderable by any reckoning, for what I have given in these pages is substantially a résumé of modern scholarship and criticism concerned with Swift. Unfortunately it has not been possible for me to indicate all of the books, articles, and reviews upon which I have drawn or which I have somehow had in mind while working out various sections of this study—the bibliography which stands at the end is a highly selective one, intended not as a record but as a help to the general reader ; and the footnotes have had to be confined to the most specific kind of references. But I am sure that my fellow scholars and critics will understand the spirit in which I have worked and the method I have here been following. I shall be happy if they will dismiss as error or obtuseness on my part anything they take exception to, if only they will acknowledge their own very considerable title to the things that seem essentially right. (I may point out that in the 1953 reprint of my longer study, *The Mind and Art of Jonathan Swift*, which first

appeared in 1936, I have given a fairly comprehensive
bibliography of Swift scholarship down to the middle of
1952.) There are certain express acknowledgements which
I must, however, make. My indebtedness to the work of
Sir Harold Williams as editor of *The Poems of Swift* and
The Journal to Stella is only less than to that of the editor
of the Shakespeare Head *Prose Works of Swift*, Professor
Herbert Davis. Anyone at all familiar with the textual and
bibliographical details afforded by their three great modern
editions will readily perceive how extensively I have used
this body of materials. Professor Davis and his publishers,
Messrs. Blackwell & Mott, were helpful quite beyond the
call of duty in making available to me, this spring, the
proofs of the forthcoming Volume XII of *The Prose Works
of Swift*. As a result I have been able to revise the eighth
chapter of my study in the light of Professor Davis's bibliographical statements concerning the Irish pamphlets of
1727-33, at the same time bringing into accord with the
Davis text several quotations from these pamphlets. I also
have Professor Louis Landa of Princeton University to
thank for letting me, with characteristic generosity, read
his book, *Swift and the Church of Ireland*, while it was still
in proof—I have called attention in several footnotes to the
new light which his monograph throws on various details
in Swift's clerical career. Finally, I want to express to the
Research Committee of the Graduate School of the University of Wisconsin and to Dean M. H. Ingraham of the
College of Letters and Science my gratitude for relieving
me of certain of my routine academic duties during the year
1953-4 in order that I might work to better advantage on
this *Introduction*.

R. Q.

Madison, Wisconsin
May 1954

CONTENTS

NOTE ON TEXTS USED
AND
ACKNOWLEDGEMENTS

By permission of editor and publisher, the text of Swift's prose used throughout this study—with the exception of a few casually-quoted phrases here and there—is that given by Mr. Herbert Davis in his edition of *The Prose Works of Jonathan Swift* (Oxford: Basil Blackwell & Mott, Ltd., 1937-[in progress]). As noted in my Preface, Mr. Davis, together with Messrs. Blackwell & Mott, kindly made available to me in the spring of 1954 the texts of the Irish pamphlets of the 1727-33 period given by Mr. Davis in the forthcoming Vol. XII of his edition.

The text of Swift's verse is taken from *The Poems of Jonathan Swift*, edited by Sir Harold Williams (3 vols.; Oxford: Clarendon Press, 1937), by permission of the Clarendon Press.

The text of the *Journal to Stella* is from the edition by Sir Harold Williams (2 vols.; Oxford: Clarendon Press, 1948), by permission of the Clarendon Press.

The text of the correspondence is taken from *The Correspondence of Jonathan Swift*, edited by F. Elrington Ball (6 vols.; G. Bell & Sons, Ltd., 1910-14), by permission of the publishers, Messrs. G. Bell & Sons, Ltd.

I take this occasion to thank all of those according me these permissions.

R. Q.

I

SWIFT'S CAREER

JONATHAN SWIFT was born on 30 November 1667 in Dublin. The Swifts had only recently settled in Ireland, having gone over soon after the Restoration—some six of them, all sons of a fiercely Royalist clergyman of Hereford-shire. The eldest of these brothers was Godwin Swift, barrister, related by marriage to the great Ormonde family and at one time holding the Attorney-Generalship of Tip-perary. Another of the brothers was Jonathan—that is, Jonathan the elder, father of the satirist—who in 1664 had married Abigail Erick, a Leicestershire girl, and had sub-sequently been appointed to a minor post as Steward of the King's Inns. Jonathan's fortunes were still to make when he suffered an untimely death in the spring of 1667. His wife, their daughter Jane (born in 1666), and the son born posthumously at the end of November 1667 thus were left dependent upon the goodwill of Godwin and the other brothers. But the Swifts in Dublin constituted a large family, now well enough established so that a proper start in life was assured to everyone, and the young Jonathan received the best education which Ireland—the Ireland of the English governing class—had to offer. In 1674 he was sent to Kilkenny School, and thereafter in the spring of 1682 to Trinity College, Dublin, where he took the degree of B.A. in February 1686. He was still in residence at Trinity College and on the point of receiving the Master's degree when violence, in the wake of England's Bloodless Revolution of 1688, broke out in Ireland, threatening Eng-lish rule and bringing normal life in Dublin to a stop. Early in 1689 Swift, along with many of his class, crossed the Irish Sea to England, where his prospects, however dim, were at least better than they could possibly be in Ireland at such a time.

The ten-year period which dates from his arrival in England was an all-important one in his development, for it was then that he came to intellectual maturity, took stock of his own situation in the world and in consequence determined upon a life in the Church, and after a none-too-successful wooing of the Muse discovered that his true vein lay in prose satire. Swift seems first to have paid a visit to his mother, who at some previous time had returned to her native Leicester to live. The close of the year, however, found him at Moor Park, Surrey, the home of Sir William Temple, the retired diplomat. The Temple family had been associated with Irish affairs since the beginning of the century, and Sir William's father, Master of the Rolls in Ireland both before and after the Restoration, had come to know Swift's uncles well. It was probably through the father, John Temple, that Swift was first brought to the attention of Sir William, who was now on the point of publishing a collection of his essays—the second such collection—and stood in need of a secretary. It was in such a capacity that Swift served Temple off and on until the latter's death in January 1699. Swift's goings and comings during these years—twice he returned to Ireland, twice he was induced to return to Moor Park—are made sufficiently clear in the correspondence which has survived from this period. His first return to Ireland occurred in May 1690 and was occasioned by a severe illness. Much later, in his fragmentary *Autobiography*, he described this illness as 'a giddiness and coldness of stomach', and went on to say that it marked the first appearance of that disorder which was to pursue him to the end of his life. It has by this time been clearly established that the disability from which he suffered for so many years was Ménière's syndrome, involving a disease of the semi-circular canals of the ears and consequent periods of giddiness, nausea, and deafness.

Swift was probably wrong in associating the illness of 1690 with his later affliction, which seems to have first struck at the end of October 1710. Thereafter, as his correspondence shows, he was subject to periodic attacks, often of great intensity.[1] On the authority of Edward Young,[2] Swift is said to have declared once, while gazing at an elm tree the upper branches of which had begun to wither, 'I shall be like that tree, (I shall die at top.') However, if Swift's own letters are evidence, it was not insanity that he dreaded, but the terrible periods of giddiness and deafness when for days at a time he was in physical torment. Labyrinthine vertigo, which in the majority of cases will yield to modern surgery, is nothing allied to madness, and is not to be confused with the physical and mental decay which overtook Swift in his old age. He remained active, we should remember, into his later sixties. Swift has often been described as one suffering from some inherent morbidity of mind and temper, but when we consider the greatness of his achievement in the face of a physical handicap which would have broken another's spirit, we are impressed by his courage and his remarkable powers of self-control and self-discipline.

Swift was in Ireland when the Battle of the Boyne was fought (1 July 1690). Temple had provided him with a letter to Sir Robert Southwell, now serving with King William in Ireland as Secretary of State, in which he had expressed the hope that a secretaryship might be found for the young Anglo-Irishman—he 'has Latin and Greek,' Temple assured Sir Robert, 'some French, writes a very good and current hand, is very honest and diligent'—or perhaps a fellowship at Trinity College. After some months,

[1] For a recent and authoritative discussion of this entire matter, see Sir Walter Russell Brain, 'The Illness of Dean Swift', *Irish Journal of Medical Science*, Sixth Series, Nos. 320-1 (August-September 1952), 337-45.

[2] See *Conjectures on Original Composition*.

during which neither secretaryship nor fellowship had been forthcoming, Swift was back at his old post at Moor Park. His second residence at Temple's lasted from December 1691 to the summer of 1694 and is memorable as the period during which he attempted with all of his as-yet-unorganized energy to make himself into a poet. Previously, in Ireland, he had composed an ode in celebration of King William's triumphs there. Odes—in the form made popular by Abraham Cowley—now continued to attract him, though towards the end of these experiments he turned to the heroic couplet. The last of these verse pieces (dated December 1693) ends with his dismissal of the Muse:

> from this hour
> I here renounce thy visionary pow'r;
> And since thy essence on my breath depends,
> Thus with a puff the whole delusion ends.

But though he found himself thwarted for the moment in his efforts at poetry, he had been gathering in a wealth of new experiences, social and intellectual. He had gone up to Oxford, been incorporated a member from Hart Hall— Temple's good offices are apparent—and received the M.A. (July 1692). He had made up his mind to take orders in the Church, but not until King William—who had high regard for Temple and sometimes consulted him in regard to English politics—gave him a prebend, as he had promised to do. It must have been in 1693 that Temple sent him up to Kensington to discuss the constitutional aspects of the Triennial Bill with the King and the royal adviser, the Earl of Portland. Swift was developing fast. The library at Moor Park was in itself a liberal education, for Temple's interests extended to travel literature, modern history, the various civilizations of the world, and letters, ancient and modern. Editorial work on Temple's essays, letters, and diplomatic memoirs was sharpening Swift's stylistic sense and giving him an understanding of how a modern and well-informed mind ranged over theories having to do with art, human culture, political behaviour, and the rise and fall of civilization. Finally, it was Moor Park that conveyed into his mind and sensibilities that social attitude characteristic of such enlightened men and women of this era as Halifax, Temple himself, and Lady Temple, the latter known to us for the charming letters which as Dorothy Osborne she wrote to her future husband. Such people were well-read and widely conversant with affairs; they were conscious of their aristocratic place in the world about them, but equally so of the levelling realities of human experience and the human body; they were not lacking in warm sentiment, but they had been born into a hard-tempered age and were consciously anti-romantic in their insistence upon a realistic appraisal of all aspects of experience. The Temples thought in terms of a society wherein men and women conversed in terms of complete equality and were assumed to be identical in intellect and emotions. It was against such a background that Swift came to know Hester, or Esther, Johnson, the step-daughter of Temple's steward. She was not more than eight years old when Swift first came from Ireland. In his own words, he 'had some share in her education, by directing what books she should read, and perpetually instructing her in the principles of honour and virtue.' Long before she became Stella (a name Swift did not use until a quarter of a century later) she would seem to have taken her place in what for him was the ideal society.

In 1694, weary in all probability of waiting for preferment in England, Swift took matters into his own hands, bade farewell to an angry Temple, and returned to Dublin, where early in the ensuing year he was admitted to Anglican orders and preferred to the prebend of Kilroot in the Cathedral of Connor. In the spring of 1695 he took up his duties in his first parish. Kilroot, which lies a few miles to the north of Belfast, presented an abrupt change from

the amenities of Moor Park. Little is known of his life
during these months in northern Ireland. If it was here,
as some believe, that he made a beginning on the prose
satire ultimately to be entitled *A Tale of a Tub*—the sections thereof concerned with 'corruptions in religion' may
well have been begun while Swift was residing in one of
the great centres of Protestant dissent—we must place at
this period his discovery of his true literary powers. By
May 1696 he had had enough of Kilroot, and with Temple
urging his return and offering 'better prospect of interest'
he settled down at Moor Park for the third and last time.
Temple's death on 27 January 1699 left Swift, as his sister
put it, 'unprovided both of friend and living', but before
the Moor Park period closed he had come into his full
powers as a prose satirist. The *Tale of a Tub*, the *Battle
of the Books*, and the *Discourse Concerning the Mechanical
Operation of the Spirit*, three satiric compositions linked
together by their common themes, were not to appear from
the press until 1704, but they were largely composed at
Moor Park during the last two and a half years of residence
there. The *Battle of the Books* was, in fact, a blow delivered
in defence of Temple, whose essay *Upon Ancient and Modern
Literature* had become the centre of a literary controversy
then in progress. True enough, these early works do not
possess the ready appeal of *Gulliver's Travels*. Nevertheless, their brilliance is not easily exaggerated. They are
triumphs of the satirist's art.

At Temple's death Swift was in his thirty-second year.
He was already a satirist of great power but since he had
published nothing of consequence was still unknown.
Nothing came of the promised preferment in England.
Accordingly he accepted a post as chaplain to the Earl of
Berkeley, who was going over to Ireland that summer as
a Lord Justice. More important, he was shortly thereafter
preferred to several livings in the Irish Church—the principal one being the vicarage of Laracor—which yielded

about £200 a year[1] and thus enabled him to get back to England at frequent intervals. The period extending down to the early autumn of 1710 falls into a regular pattern: he was often at Laracor and the neighbouring town of Trim; he was well-known at Dublin Castle when Berkeley was Lord Justice and during the ensuing viceroyalties of the Duke of Ormonde and the Earl of Pembroke; and on four occasions he was in England, once for a period of over a year and a half. He wrote some verse and a good deal of prose. His authorship of the *Tale of a Tub*, published anonymously in 1704, came to be generally recognized among men of letters. His chief success, however, was scored in the *rôle* of Isaac Bickerstaff, who amused all London for the better part of two seasons.

It was during the longest of these sojourns in England (November 1707 to June 1709) that he undertook to act in behalf of the Church of Ireland in an effort to procure from the Crown certain financial benefits similar to those recently bestowed on the English Establishment. Swift's churchmanship, henceforth to play so vital a part in his career, came to be unmistakably evinced in the course of this episode. He had always regarded himself as a good Whig—in the post-Restoration era there were few Anglo-Irish who did not—and his training at Moor Park had confirmed him in political principles of a thoroughly Whiggish cast. Indeed, Swift was later to insist that he had steadfastly remained 'what they called a Whig in politics'. When, however, it became apparent to him early in 1708 that the Godolphin Ministry, originally almost entirely Tory, was now ready to win the support of extreme Whigs and of Dissenters by backing the repeal of the Test Act, and that compliance with such a policy was to be made the price of any further favours to the Church, Swift balked. Henceforth, though he retained all of his Whig theories of

[1] See Louis A. Landa, *Swift and the Church of Ireland* (Oxford, 1954), pp. 36, 42, 43.

B

government and accepted wholeheartedly the principles of the Revolution of 1688, his attitude in all matters affecting the status of the established religion was that of the High Churchman. His repeated visits to England had unquestionably been made with a view to securing a church living there rather than in Ireland. His hopes seemed to be well founded, for he had served the Whigs effectively with his pen and had brought himself to the attention of powerful men like Somers and Burnet. But if their favour depended upon falling in with measures which he could only view as hostile to the Church, he was prepared to sever his ties with the party to which he looked for advancement. When he returned to Ireland at the end of June 1709 he had yet to take an open stand against the Whigs, but he had written more than one pamphlet in defence of the Church.

Most of the writing which Swift did in the course of these eleven years between January 1699 and September 1710 was occasional. There was more than a little verse, much of it interesting, some of it first-rate. There were humorous prose pieces like the *Meditation on a Broomstick* and the Partridge papers. There were pamphlets concerned with current events in the political field and in the area where secular and church interests met. In this body of writing Swift was displaying further aspects of his now thoroughly-matured powers. Though he had once renounced poetry, he now proved to be an accomplished writer of informal verse of a witty and ironical cast. As a humorist he found great delight—and gave as much— in masquerading in the guise of such imagined characters as the author of the *Meditation on a Broomstick* and Isaac Bickerstaff. In 1701 he had first come forward as a pamphlet writer. The occasion was the attempted impeachment of Somers and other Whig leaders by the Tory House of Commons. Swift's piece, the *Contests and Dissensions in Athens and Rome*, was both an able statement of the situation from the point of view of Whig political theory and an

effective warning to the Tories: the tone was perfectly calculated; the style—markedly different from the highly
figurative prose of the *Tale of a Tub*—was firm, straightforward, engagingly reasonable. His resourcefulness in this
kind of writing was demonstrated again in the pamphlets
which he had in hand in 1708 and 1709. He felt the need
of defining his own position as a Whig who was also a
devoted Churchman, and this he did in the *Sentiments of a
Church-of-England Man*. At the same time he was taking
up other matters relating to religion, ironically in the *Argument against Abolishing Christianity*, with straightforward
seriousness in his *Project for the Advancement of Religion and
the Reformation of Manners*. It was his plan to publish these
in a single volume and his friend Steele had agreed to
furnish a preface, but only the *Project* saw the light at this
time (April 1709). Meanwhile, alarmed by further changes
in the Ministry which seemed to presage ill for the Church,
he had written and issued his *Letter Concerning the Sacramental Test* (December 1708). In the age of pamphleteers,
few ever approached Swift in force and adroitness.

His social life had also assumed a pattern. Once, in a
moment of youthful recklessness, he had proposed marriage to a girl by the name of Jane Waring—he called her
'Varina'—whom he had come to know while serving at
Kilroot. We can still read the letter he wrote her in the
spring of 1696 as he was on the point of departure for
Moor Park. He offered to cancel all his plans if she would
have him; if she refused, she would lose him forever. A
strange composition it is, but doubtless sincere. Varina,
however, was not to be moved, and Swift left Kilroot to
rejoin Temple. Once out of Ireland he may well have made
the discovery that his emotions as a suitor had scarcely
been as profound as he had fancied, and he seems to have
forgotten Varina quickly enough. Four years later, however, after his return to Ireland as Berkeley's chaplain and
his appointment to Laracor, she re-entered his life, but only

long enough to suffer the coldest of repulses. Of the letters which must have passed between them in the spring of 1700 only Swift's has been preserved. He did not positively refuse the marriage which she now welcomed, but the terms and conditions he laid down were impossible ones for a woman with any pride. Varina is heard of no more.

It would seem that Swift, if he still considered marriage, had come to think of it in the realistic and social terms which Moor Park had taught him, and for an Irish vicar with only a small income and as yet no distinction this could only mean indefinite postponement. Something of the atmosphere of Moor Park was re-created for him in Ireland when Esther Johnson and Rebecca Dingley decided to settle there in 1700 or 1701. Rebecca Dingley was some fifteen years older than Stella, a relative of Temple's, and had made her home at Moor Park. The two women were now inseparable companions. Once in 1708 they apparently returned to England for a visit, but with this exception they were to live for the rest of their lives in Ireland. They saw Swift almost daily ; when he was in England, there was regular correspondence. But it was always Esther and Dingley whom he addressed in his letters, always Esther and Dingley with whom he dined and visited in Laracor, Trim, and Dublin. Whether Swift ever married Stella or ever thought of marrying her are questions that cannot be answered, and we have no certain knowledge of what passed in Stella's mind. How Swift felt in 1704 is pretty clear from the letter he wrote to an acquaintance of his, the Rev. William Tisdall, who had made unsuccessful advances to Stella and believed that it was Swift who was standing in his way. Swift protested that this was not the case ; true, if his fortunes and humour served him to think of marriage, he would choose Esther among all persons on earth— 'I never saw that person whose conversation I entirely valued but hers.' She was free to marry whom she would, and marriage was, indeed, held a necessary and convenient thing for ladies, since 'time takes off from the lustre of virgins in all other eyes but mine.' Swift never forgave Tisdall for his temerity—the last entry in the *Journal to Stella* contains a characteristically slighting reference to him—but it does not follow that his contempt was in the nature of what we commonly mean by jealousy. In the case of Swift and Stella we are confronted with a relationship which must be approached with something bordering upon historical imagination. It is really Swift's social sentiment, rooted in an age consciously anti-romantic, that goes furthest in explaining his attitude and probably Stella's too, since he had helped to form her character. It would scarcely have occurred to him any more than it did to someone like Lord Halifax that marriage was a peculiarly desirable thing or could ever be idyllic. Friendship was more necessary— a complex social pattern, but one which once established suffered little change.

That Swift's personality was at this time thoroughly social in the broader sense was illustrated many times both in Dublin and London. As Berkeley's chaplain he was sometimes the satirist but oftener the irrepressible humorist, and it was then that he formed a lasting friendship with Lady Betty Berkeley, the Earl's daughter. Later, in the days of Pembroke's Lord Lieutenancy, we find Swift again taking his ease at the Castle and still the humorist. When in England he assumed for a while a graver *rôle*, and it was as a political writer that he first came to the public's attention in 1701. But by the time he settled down in London late in 1707 for his protracted visit he was known to many as the author of the *Tale of a Tub*, and his reputation for wit and drollery came to be fully established in the course of the following months as a result of the Bickerstaff affair. He had become a well-known man of letters, a friend of Addison, Steele, and the other Whig writers of their circle. Before he left London early in May 1709 he had helped Steele get the *Tatler* under way, and had contributed

to the ninth number of the new journal the verses entitled
A Description of the Morning. Our impression of Swift
throughout the period under discussion is of one who
moved easily in all societies and was in high spirits most
of the time.

On the last day of August 1710 Swift again sailed for
England, landing the following day and arriving in London
on 7 September. He was at the threshold of the most
dramatic period in his career. London was astir with excitement, for the great political upheaval which saw Godolphin's
Whig Ministry replaced by the Tory Ministry of Harley
and St. John was now in progress, the coming general elec-
tion was to assure the Tories of the control of the House of
Commons, and the drive for peace—since the beginning
of Anne's reign in 1702 England and her allies had been
at war with France—was about to get under way. Swift
had again been empowered by the Irish bishops to act in
the matter of the First Fruits, regarding which he had
negotiated unsuccessfully with the Whig Ministry during
his previous visit. He resumed his old ways, talked with
important—and now disgruntled—Whigs, saw much of
Addison and Steele, and contributed to the *Tatler* a paper
on English style and a second poem, the *Description of a
City Shower.* Soon, however, the astute Harley saw to it
that he and Swift met. Harley, charming and ingratiating,
promised a speedy remission of the First Fruits. By the
end of October Swift had gone over to the Tories and had
taken up the editorship of their weekly paper, the *Examiner.*
His association with the Ministry, which became closer as
time passed, was to remain unbroken down to the *débâcle*
which overtook the Tory party at the Queen's death in
August 1714.

Swift's activities and much of the colour and movement
of the London scene during these years live vividly in the
pages of the *Journal to Stella.* Despite the traditional title
given to the best-known of all Swift's letters, they were

written to both Dingley and Esther. They began on 2 September 1710, immediately after Swift's arrival in England,
and with certain interruptions were continued down to
6 June 1713. With his two friends in Ireland Swift could
drop all reserve, and his phrasing and his orthography were
both designed to create the illusion of conversation. He
sent them the latest news from the political front; he kept
them informed of his journalistic activities; he gave them
accounts of his social experiences, amusing, gratifying, dis-
agreeable; he confided in them regarding his relations with
the ministers and his hopes for better church preferment.
What with the *Journal*, the rest of his correspondence, and
the prose and verse which he produced during these years
—the 'four last years of the Queen's reign'—we are able
to follow him not only in act but to a large degree in motive.
In his first entry in the *Journal* he had confessed that he
had never come to England with so little desire. That is,
his previously unsuccessful negotiations over the First
Fruits, the attitude of the Godolphin Ministry towards the
Test Act, and his own failure to better his circumstances
still rankled; and as yet the new disposition of affairs had
not fully disclosed itself. Arrived in London, he found the
Whigs 'ravished' to see him—but promising him nothing
against the future. His rapid conversion to the Tories came
almost inevitably. By the immediate promise of favourable
action on the First Fruits Harley convinced him that the
Tory party was indeed the Church party. Quite as important, Harley seems to have persuaded him once and for
all that the new Ministry was the instrument of no partisan
group but of all reasonable men—Swift might act the High
Churchman to the top of his bent without surrendering a
single one of his Revolution principles. That Swift was
now to yield himself up to the spirit of virulent partisanship does not alter certain facts: namely that Harley, the
trimmer by nature, was not entirely misrepresenting his
own view of the Ministry at the outset of its career; and

that Swift remained convinced to the end of his days that Harley and the others in power were as free of Jacobitism and as loyal to the Revolution settlement as he. Of Harley's and St. John's secret correspondence with the Pretender Swift knew nothing. Implicitly he believed that the entire course of action which as the chief Tory journalist he came to interpret so plausibly was in keeping with the maintenance of both the Established Church and the political tradition of 1689.

Of the vast amount of writing which he undertook as Tory journalist and apologist during these memorable four years, we can readily distinguish two varieties. In the pages of the *Examiner* (written by Swift from early November 1710 until mid-June 1711), in his party pamphlet, *The Conduct of the Allies* (December 1711), in such tracts as *Some Advice to the October Club* (January 1712) and the *Letter to a Whig Lord* (June 1712), and in the *History of the Four Last Years of the Queen* (composed in 1712 and 1713 with immediate publication in mind, but never printed during Swift's life) he was addressing the public in clear, forthright terms: he defended the Ministry, he summarized complex situations and problems to show that the line being taken was in every way the necessary and desirable one, he pleaded for support, from time to time he lashed out in invective, always he argued on grounds of reason and common sense. Here the great events of the era stand forth in ordered terms. France had now been virtually defeated and the nation was weary of the war. The Tories had come to power committed to finding a way of making peace. Negotiations with Louis had been undertaken, but it was not until the closing day of 1711 that victory for the ministerial policy was assured in Parliament. Even then the formal terms of peace had still to be worked out between the English, her allies, and Louis's representatives. This proved to be a matter of long negotiation, and it was not until the spring of 1713 that the Treaty of Utrecht was finally signed.

Through 1711, first in the *Examiner* and then in the *Conduct of the Allies*, Swift was whipping up support for the Tory peace policy. The triumph of this policy as a result of parliamentary events which came to a head at the year's end did not mean, however, that the political battle was over. The negotiations at Utrecht, prolonged through 1712, afforded Whigs on the one hand and overly zealous Tories on the other many opportunities to build up resentment against the Ministry, and Swift's services continued to be effective in explaining the measures afoot and urging co-operation with Harley and St. John (now, respectively, the Earl of Oxford and Viscount Bolingbroke).

But not all of his politically inspired writing was of this order. Swift's roots lay in the Restoration era, and like the writers of that period he had an irrepressible instinct for the lampoon and the scurrilous pamphlet. Without condoning his many libellous attacks in verse and prose—that, indeed, is often impossible—we may nevertheless recognize the tradition he was drawing upon and the techniques which went with it. Always anonymous, he would sometimes, especially in his prose pamphlets, deliver his attack or perpetrate his hoax under some assumed character. Shortly after his arrival in London he had paid his respects to Godolphin, the late Whig minister, in the insulting verses of *The Virtues of Sid Hamet the Magician's Rod* (September 1710). He afterwards lampooned both the Duchess of Somerset and Marlborough in verse, and reviled Wharton in a *Short Character*: their sins were various but they were all Whigs. In a short prose piece like the *Letter of Thanks from Wharton* (July 1712) we observe how devastatingly he could employ satiric impersonation.

It was not until April 1713 that Swift received any reward for his service to the party in power. He had never asked for a penny, it being understood from the first that church preferment alone was in question. No less than three English deaneries had now fallen vacant, and Swift

began to press his case with Oxford and Bolingbroke—
from the Moor Park days he had dreamt of preferment in
England. But when matters came to be finally arranged,
he found that he had been given the Deanery of St. Patrick's
in Dublin. To be sure, it was a post that carried with it
much prestige and a satisfactory income, but as he expressed
it in the *Journal*, he could not feel joy at passing his days in
Ireland; 'and I confess,' he added, 'I thought the Ministry
would not let me go; but perhaps they cant help it.' The
entries in the *Journal* for April 1713 give a vivid account
of the day-to-day negotiations concerning the various
deaneries, Swift's long suspense, and his final disappoint-
ment. All that went on behind the scenes is still not clear.
Swift had made many enemies, and there were undoubtedly
those who had persuaded themselves that the author of a
Tale of a Tub could not be a sincere and worthy clergyman.[1]
In the poem entitled *The Author upon Himself*, written a
year after the events, Swift attributed his being kept in
Ireland to the enmity of Queen Anne—set against him by
the Duchess of Somerset—and to Sharp, the Archbishop
of York.

June saw Swift in Dublin, being installed as Dean. It
was not long, however, before he was summoned back to
London. While the strength of the Tories was being sapped
by divided counsels, a breach of long standing between
Oxford and Bolingbroke was becoming critical, and those
who were closest to the two warring ministers felt that it
was Swift who stood the best chance of bringing about a
reconciliation. He arrived in London early in September,
once more to assume the *rôle* of Tory publicist. All friendship between him and Steele had now been killed off by

---

[1] Swift's appointment seems, in fact, to have displeased Tories and High
Churchmen quite as much as it did the Whigs. Robert Molesworth, prominent in Irish affairs, who happened to be in London at this time, reported
that it had vexed 'the godly party beyond expression' (quoted by Louis
Landa, op. cit., p. xv).

the excessive partisanship which moved both men, and when Steele voiced his fears of Toryism and Jacobitism Swift retorted. *The Importance of the Guardian Considered* (October 1713) and *The Public Spirit of the Whigs* (February 1714) were his final and most strident political pamphlets under the Tory Ministry. In the meantime the situation which he had come over to remedy had gone from bad to worse. In despair of Ministry and party, and dreading what inevitably lay in store in the event of the Queen's death, obviously not far off, he retired in May to a friend's country parsonage in Berkshire. Awaiting the end of the drama, he found relief in summing matters up in *Some Free Thoughts Upon the Present State of Affairs*. Here in Berkshire he also composed two notable poems of retrospection, *The Author upon Himself* and the imitation of Horace's *Hoc erat in votis* ('I often wish'd, that I had clear'). The Queen's death on 1 August ended an era. The ensuing one belonged to the Whigs. Before the end of that month Swift had retired to the Deanery in Dublin, exhausted by work and shrinking from a world now in the complete possession of the enemy.

Swift was then forty-six. There followed an interval of some five years of comparative inactivity, during which he lived in seclusion, occupying himself with the affairs of the Cathedral and observing the new political scene with a studied indifference. By 1719, however, there were signs that his restless energy was returning. The ensuing decade, the most remarkable of his whole career, saw his emergence as Irish patriot, the publication of the *Drapier's Letters* and *Gulliver's Travels*, and the composition of much of his finest verse. Swift's powers were somewhat late in maturing, but contrary to the popular myth they were long sustained: he was almost fifty-nine when *Gulliver's Travels* appeared, in his sixties when he wrote some of his most effective poems, and just short of seventy at the time of his final agitation in behalf of Ireland's interests. The years in Ireland extending from 1714 to his death in 1745 constitute a long period marked by the highest achievement, the more remarkable when we consider his utter discouragement at the start, the recurrent periods of illness, and the nature of the political scene throughout.

Writing to Bolingbroke in September 1714, he described his new circumstances: 'I live a country life in town, see nobody, and go every day once to prayers.' His thoughts lay in the past. In October he was engaged upon the *Memoirs Relating to That Change Which Happened in the Queen's Ministry in the Year 1710*; the *Enquiry into the Behaviour of the Queen's Last Ministry* was begun in June 1715, following the flight of Bolingbroke and Ormonde to the continent and the imprisonment of Oxford, events brought on by the inquiry on the part of the new Parliament into the Jacobite intrigue. Swift remained unshaken in his conviction that the Tory ministers were guiltless of the charges being made against them. In July 1715 he wrote to Oxford, then in the Tower, to make 'the humblest offers' of his 'poor service and attendance', and before Oxford's acquittal in 1717 he addressed him in the poem *To the Earl of Oxford, Late Lord Treasurer*.

Gradually Swift's circle of acquaintances began to widen, and important friendships were formed with such people as Chetwode, Delany, and Thomas Sheridan. But a shadow lay over these years—a shadow cast by the presence in Ireland of Esther Vanhomrigh. Born in Ireland of Dutch descent, she was younger than Stella by some seven years. After her father's death she had gone with her mother and the rest of the family to London, where Swift came to know her during his visit of 1707-1709. Later, in the period which saw him established as Tory journalist, Swift made the Vanhomrighs' house a sort of headquarters, and it was there that the friendship between him and Vanessa, as he called her, was firmly established. However, by the time he left for Dublin in June 1713 to be installed as Dean friendship on Vanessa's part had changed to something else, as the letters which passed between them that summer show clearly enough. *Cadenus and Vanessa*, Swift's version of their story up to that time—a version designed to resolve all difficulties into high comedy—was probably written after his return to England that autumn. But the later chapters of their story were to exclude the comic Muse. When Swift took up permanent residence in Ireland after the Queen's death, Vanessa followed him. His attempts to dissuade her from doing so, his efforts as the years passed to keep a proper distance between them, her passion, her despair at his aloofness—these are recorded in the surviving portions of their remarkable correspondence. That Swift was thoughtless or injudicious during the earlier years of their acquaintance may have been the case; but anyone who reads their letters must feel sympathy for both of them: for Vanessa because of her uncontrollable passion; for Swift by reason of the position he found himself in, unmoved save by friendship and his compassion at another's suffering. The last of their extant letters date from 1722. Thereafter a break is believed to have occurred. Vanessa died in June 1723, and Swift, to escape evil tongues, left on a long journey through the south of Ireland. To what extent his relations with Stella were affected by what passed between him and Vanessa is hard to tell. Did Stella take offence? In 1716 did she, indeed, insist upon a marriage —a marriage in name only, but at least an assurance that the friendship between her and Swift would be sustained despite Vanessa? Such is the story that has often been told and often denied. The evidence that a secret marriage ceremony was performed—if there was a marriage, it was admittedly only a ceremony—is inconclusive. Stella and Vanessa would seem to have represented for Swift different aspects of social experience, Stella the cultivated, dignified life that accorded with well-defined position, Vanessa—that is at the beginning of their acquaintance—the amusing excitements of an *ingénue* and the comedy of the world as she pictured it. It is tragically clear that Vanessa was unable to accept the *rôle* created for her : there is little to indicate that Stella ever wanted to change hers.

It is significant that the renewal of Swift's purely literary impulses coincided with his emergence as a public figure and the beginning of his agitation in behalf of the Irish interest. To 1719 may be assigned a group of poems which includes the remarkable *Progress of Beauty*. Not long after came the *Letter to a Young Gentleman, Lately entr'd into Holy Orders* (1720), and the *Letter to a Young Lady, on her Marriage* (1723).[1] The latter, written in the tradition of Halifax's *Advice to a Daughter* and expressive of Swift's own anti-romantic sentiments ('. . . I hope, you do not still dream of Charms and Raptures ; which Marriage ever did, and ever will put a sudden End to'), has a biographical importance which should not be overlooked, for no assessment of Swift's personal life is acceptable which does not accord with the tone and social temper of this characteristic statement of his. Much happened in 1720 that helped to set Swift's future course of action. The bursting of the South Sea Bubble in August did not bring about the fall of the Whigs, but it did give Swift an opening, which as Patriot Dean he proceeded to exploit to the full. In common with all the Anglo-Irish he was deeply stung by the passing early in 1720 of the 'Act for the better securing the Dependency of the Kingdom of Ireland upon the Crown of Great Britain', and the first in his great series of Irish pamphlets, the *Proposal for the Universal Use of Irish Manufacture*, was now written. Its publication in May 1720 was set to coincide with the celebration of King George's birthday, and was clear warning that in Ireland the Tory opposition had donned the robes of patriotism.

Four years later Swift was leading the battle against

1 Swift's authorship of the *Letter of Advice to a Young Poet* (1721) is now in question. See Herbert Davis, *The Prose Works of Swift*, IX, xxiv f.

Wood's halfpence. A scarcity of coins in Ireland had prompted the authorities in London to issue a patent, which had been secured by William Wood, providing for the mintage of copper halfpence and farthings for circulation in Ireland. When news of the patent reached Dublin there was immediate opposition on the part of the Commissioners of Revenue, and before the close of 1723 both houses of the Irish Parliament had sent Addresses to the King. Modern historians have no difficulty in showing that the feeling of alarm throughout Ireland was justified by past experience as well as by certain of the terms of the new patent. Swift did not fabricate a specious case against England and the government of Walpole. The case was a strong one, and it was there before he took it up. The *Drapier's Letters* came out in 1724 at a time of tremendous excitement, the first in March, the second and third in August, the fourth —*A Letter to the Whole People of Ireland*—just as Carteret, the new Lord Lieutenant sent over to take command of the situation, was landing. Swift wrote three more *Letters*, though two of them were withheld until much later; but the tide had turned against Wood, and in August 1725 the Irish were informed that the patent had been surrendered. Swift had brought his fellow-countrymen together in a common cause. To be sure, they were all English, these fellow-countrymen—the native Irish scarcely figured —but not all were Anglican and fewer still were Tories.

Swift's greatest satire was written in the midst of these activities. Before the death of the Queen a number of the Tory men of letters had formed what came to be known as the Scriblerus Club. The members were Swift, Arbuthnot, Parnell, Pope, and Gay; the Earl of Oxford, though he did not qualify in point of authorship, was sometimes present. The chief project undertaken by the group was a satiric biography of an imaginary hero, Martinus Scriblerus, whom they loaded with most of the traditional intellectual follies. It is quite possibly in this connexion that Swift's mind was first turned, early in 1714, to a series of imaginary voyages, for it had apparently been decided that Martin was to travel to various strange lands and report his observations there. However this may be, we know from his letters to Charles Ford that he had begun work on *Gulliver's Travels* by 1721, and we learn of the order in which the four parts of the satire were composed: Parts I and II were finished by the end of 1723; by January 1724 he had written the fourth voyage and was at work on the third; revisions and transcription of the whole were finished before the end of September 1725 (though evidence outside the letters suggests that a certain amount of new material may have been incorporated between this last date and publication in October 1726). Whatever else it may be, *Gulliver's Travels* is not the work of an introverted recluse. It was written in the midst of the excitement and distractions of a great public campaign.

Swift returned to England only twice in the years following the Queen's death, in 1726 and 1727. The occasion of the first visit was his desire to arrange for the publication of the now-completed *Gulliver's Travels*. He crossed early in March, and on arrival in London was met by Pope and afterwards by Arbuthnot, Pulteney, Bolingbroke, and Gay. Since it was both a reunion of the Scriblerus Club and a forgathering of notable Tory malcontents, literature and politics entered largely into their conversations and their plans. Swift visited Bolingbroke at Dawley, near Uxbridge, and then joined Pope at Twickenham. The Drapier's presence in England had been duly noted by the government, and in April Swift and Walpole dined together. Swift reported shortly afterwards, in a letter to his friend, the Earl of Peterborough, that he had tried to set the chief minister right regarding the status of Ireland but had failed in his design. What purpose Walpole had had in mind is not known, though he may have been led to believe that Swift was ready for conversion. Nothing was further from the truth, as forthcoming events demonstrated. Meanwhile preparation for the publication of *Gulliver's Travels* went forward. Pope, Gay, Arbuthnot, and other friends seem to have had a part in putting the finishing touches to the satire and in devising the elaborate stratagem as a result of which the publisher Benjamin Motte, after negotiations with an unknown 'Richard Sympson', came into possession of the full copy in manuscript. Swift was safely back in Dublin when the book appeared on 28 October. It enjoyed a great and immediate success, the talk it occasioned being duly reported to Swift by his friends in London.

Swift's second and final visit—in 1727—likewise involved both literature and politics. He and Pope were now laying plans for their joint *Miscellanies*, four volumes of which were eventually to appear (Volumes I and II before the end of June 1727; the 'Last Volume' in March 1728; 'Volume III' in 1732). Pope's *Dunciad*—to be published in its first form in May 1728—was taking shape, and Gay's masterpiece, *The Beggar's Opera*, was to have its initial performance in January 1728. In the field of political journalism Bolingbroke, under the name of the 'Occasional Writer', was now writing in the Tory journal, the *Craftsman*. In May Swift was confiding to Sheridan that the Tory group had entered upon 'a firm settled resolution to assault the present administration, and break it if possible.' But their plans and hopes soon came to nothing, for when George I died in June it was at once apparent that Walpole's Ministry was to be just as strongly entrenched under George II.

Swift was depressed as he made his way back to Ireland not merely because he now understood the full strength of the Whigs but also for reasons deeply personal. For some time Stella had been in ill health. During his English visit of the previous year, when it was already clear that she did not have long to live, he had mentioned their long relationship to friends in Ireland: 'We have been perfect friends these thirty-five years'; 'I am of opinion there is not a

c

greater folly than to contract too great and intimate a friendship, which must always leave the survivor miserable'; '. . . I know not what I am saying; but believe me that violent friendship is much more lasting, and as much engaging, as violent love'. Stella's death occurred on 28 January 1728. We have, among other things, Swift's *Prayer for Stella* and his account of her entitled *On the Death of Mrs. Johnson*, begun the evening of her death.

If the best of life was now over for him, there was much work still to be done. He was not only the greatest man of letters in Ireland, but the foremost Irish patriot, and the most distinguished and vehemently articulate Churchman. He had his duties as Dean to perform and all the routine business pertaining to his Chapter to look after, and as has recently been pointed out the political divisions of this period were reflected within the Cathedral in such a pronounced fashion that Swift was never able to enjoy complete peace within his own domain.[1] The pamphlets he issued in behalf of Ireland's interests include *A Short View of the State of Ireland* (1728), *An Answer To A Paper, Called 'A Memorial of the poor Inhabitants, Tradesmen, and Labourers of the Kingdom of Ireland'* (1728), *A Modest Proposal* (1729), and the *Proposal for Giving Badges to the Beggars* (1737). As a Churchman he warred with the Bishops whenever it appeared to him that they had designs upon the inferior clergy, with the Presbyterians whenever an attempt was made to repeal the existing laws which penalized Dissent in Ireland, and with the Irish House of Commons whenever they showed sympathy for proposed anti-clerical legislation. In his numerous charities and in his constant service on many of Dublin's charitable committees he was both Patriot and Churchman. Finally, the period which brought forth *A Modest Proposal* was by no means barren in letters. The amusing *Directions to Servants* and *Polite Conversation* date from the '30s. He produced such notable poems as

[1] See Louis Landa, op. cit., p. 91.

the *Journal of a Modern Lady* (1729), the *Lady's Dressing Room* (1730), *Verses on the Death of Dr. Swift* (1731), *The Beast's Confession* (1732), and the politically inspired *Epistle to a Lady* (1733) and *On Poetry: A Rhapsody* (1733). The last of his satires, directed against the Irish House of Commons, is the *Legion Club*, written in 1736. At his birthday that autumn, as he entered his seventieth year, there was a celebration that extended throughout Dublin. His powers were failing, but six more years were to pass before his mind gave way. In August 1742 he was found of unsound mind and incapable of caring for himself. He died on 19 October 1745 and was buried in St. Patrick's Cathedral, next to Stella and beneath the famous epitaph which he himself had composed.

II

ASPECTS OF SWIFT

If the history of Swift commentary and criticism makes anything clear, it is assuredly this : misinterpretation of one degree or another is unavoidable unless as man and writer he is approached in terms of his historical period and the patterns of thought and behaviour which characterized it. However, before turning our attention to the contexts which most readily explain his development and his mature mind and character, we should do well to consider, as briefly as possible, the Swift of popular myth. As Dublin's foremost citizen his private life was long subject to the distortions of gossip and rumour, and later literary history was not always careful to distinguish between ascertainable fact and legend. It is true that the sensational nature of much of this legend does undoubtedly reflect something of Swift's own genius for the dramatic attitude and phrase. We must, nevertheless, be on guard against the misconstructions which have so often been placed upon his character and the intent of his satire. He has been portrayed in exaggerated terms as an egoist driven by desire for self-expression and emotional release, and betrayed into an all-embracing pessimism by personal disappointments. His physical disabilities have been unduly dwelt upon, and it has been implied if not openly stated that some form of insanity was present from the beginning. Incipient madness, or if not that something close to it, a failure of nerve, of desire, has been found at the heart of his greatest satires. His relations with Stella and Vanessa, the subject of curiosity from the time of the latter's death right down to our own day, have not only been given a prominence which has tended to obscure the fact that all the other major episodes in his life took

place entirely outside the realm of sentiment ; they have
been treated, time and again, in a spirit which has encouraged the wildest flights of fancy. There is the old story,
for instance, that Swift learned to his horror, directly after
his marriage to Stella, that they were half-brother and -sister,
and we are asked to accept as fact the conjecture that Swift
and Esther Johnson were both natural children of Sir
William Temple. There is the new story—place of origin :
Dublin ; year : 1938—according to which Esther remains
Temple's natural daughter but Swift becomes the natural
son of Temple's father and thus Esther's half-uncle instead
of half-brother. All this is sheer romancing, for a marriage
between Swift and Stella remains unproved, the story concerning Temple being Stella's father has been investigated
and found quite unsubstantiated by fact, and Swift's traditional parentage can scarcely be called in question save by
a process of reasoning which would leave most of us in
doubt about our own legitimacy. In the previous chapter
the more important facts of Swift's life have been set forth.
These show us a Swift who was many-sided, of great energy,
who rarely shrank into himself ; one who laid great emphasis
upon friendship, combining sociability and the hard, anti-
romantic temper acquired during youth. Taken by themselves, these facts do not suggest the need of anything
particularly sensational in the way of interpretation. They
give us a picture which is reasonably complete and consistent.

Since Freud the popular myth that we have been speaking
of has tended to become what might be called a psychiatric
myth. The basic assumptions remain the same : Swift suffered in life from frustrations which warped his character
and his work. But a new and exciting vocabulary, with
emphasis upon sexual difficulties and a fear of life inter-
preted as the death impulse, supplants the older terminology.
Those who find the resulting analysis of Swift plausible are
not usually disposed to argue the matter save on grounds
of their own choosing, any more than are the critics who

rest content with the assumption that Swift's satiric art is essentially a matter of unconscious self-revelation. (No one could very well take the position that Swift was without eccentricities,) that there were no curious elements in his make-up or strange episodes in his life, or that his genius is to be flattened out into the commonplace. But one may concede a great deal and still insist upon a view which rests, biographically, upon the known facts, and critically upon the conviction that literature is better discussed in terms of its own artistic being than of what we may choose to believe to have been the author's subjective experience. In the end, no matter what course we have pursued, our understanding of people no less than of works of art and of historical epochs must remain a matter of intuition. There is, however, all the difference in the world between what sometimes passes for intuition in these matters and that understanding which is arrived at through discrimination and deliberate assessment.

The charge brought against Swift in our own day, notably by George Orwell, stands somewhat differently.[1] Among other things it introduces certain historical elements into the picture by way of Swift's social and intellectual views, and though it still does not bring us to the kind of historical explorations and definitions which will be taken up presently, it concerns a very important aspect of Swift and must be taken into account. The charge amounts to this: Swift preached a closed society. Though that precise term is not used by Orwell, we are told that Swift's values and world-view were those of a reactionary who had come to believe that ordinary life is not worth living; democracy repelled him, intellectual curiosity excited his scorn. Orwell's statement is cogent—all the more so because of his high estimate of Swift's literary qualities—and there are probably a good many readers who will feel that it is

[1] I refer to Orwell's essay, 'Politics vs. Literature: An Examination of "Gulliver's Travels" ', in *Shooting an Elephant and other Essays* (1950).

essentially right. But it invites inspection. In his magnificent essay on Swift which preceded Orwell's by some years, W. B. Yeats had as a matter of fact anticipated this line of attack and had suggested one way to handle it.[1] In Yeats's view there was a force in Swift that becomes intelligible only when seen as the function of a specific moment in history. Swift was indeed the spokesman of a domineering society—that society set up by the Protestant aristocracy in Ireland after the Revolution of 1688—and his character and works express both the wisdom and the arrogance which came to one so situated. To understand him, therefore, is to accept his *données*, with no questions asked how he fits into any present set of values : he is one of those great figures whom we should see as if time were 'broken away from their feet'.

Whatever else we are inclined to make of Yeats's statement, we have to acknowledge that it is the clearest sort of challenge to those whose method of judging historical figures consists of bringing them into the present and placing them in modern situations. It is not easy to transplant a mind from the past—even from the not-so-remote past of Swift's age—to the twentieth century. When we declare that Swift had no love of democracy, what precisely do we mean? That he would have been a fascist in the 1930s? It seems unlikely that anyone could seriously envisage the Drapier Dean in any such *rôle*. Before we can say what his political principles would turn out to be were they to operate in the modern world we must go through an exacting process of historical extrapolation. I believe, however, a great many people who honour Swift's memory are going to insist that, necessary as it is to see him in historical context, it is next to impossible to keep one of his energy of mind and character perpetually confined in the past. They will incline,

[1] The essay in question is the Introduction to the play, *The Words upon the Window-Pane*, produced in 1930. Introduction and play were given in *Wheels and Butterflies* (1934).

with Orwell, towards some translation into modern terms, though many of them will take issue with Orwell's main findings. For instance, there would seem to be some carry-over in the matter of political theory. More will be said of Swift's political thought in later chapters. Here it will suffice to call attention to the concept of freedom which he defended with Roman eloquence. His positive principles were those of the seventeenth-century jurists and parliamentarians who had fought the absolutist theories of the Stuarts. Though the ideas of equality, economic, social, and political, which have arisen in modern industrial society were all foreign to his mind, the doctrines he upheld have an indisputable place in the tradition of liberal political thought which has flowed into the present from sources in the seventeenth century and earlier. The Drapier may not have been speaking for the whole of Ireland—though most of Ireland seemed to think that he was—but the thunderous accusations of tyranny which he directed at Walpole's government have refused to remain mere Anglo-Irish manifestoes. It is to be said, further, that there is still a place in modern democratic society for the voice raised, not for egalitarianism, but against engulfing mediocrity. Swift's satire of critics without taste, pedants without imagination, and scientific experimenters without common sense has more than one face. Malice there may have been, but it was informed malice. Swift invoked the rights and privileges of a small and enlightened class of society—a class whose obligation it was to make everlasting war against the innumerable forms of stupidity which the Augustan wits summed up in the single word *dulness*. Orwell chose to see only the air of superiority, the hostility to genuine effort, which mark Swift's ridicule of various forms of intellectual endeavour. But if Swift spoke for a group, it was not, after all, one which carried much influence in everyday affairs during the reigns of the first two Georges. Even in the eighteenth century it was minority opinion that he and his fellow satirists were voicing. Today it could very well be less than that. Can one doubt that Swift would insist upon his right as a free and rational individual to make sport of anything which struck him as intellectual nonsense, however sanctified by prevailing opinion? Talking with Dr. Arbuthnot, the Princess of Wales once praised Swift's wit and good conversation. Arbuthnot replied that that was not what he valued Swift for, 'but for being a sincere honest man, and speaking truth when others were afraid to speak it.'

To turn, now, to the more strictly historical aspects. We commonly think of Swift as an eighteenth-century figure, forgetting that his roots lay in the previous era of the Restoration. It is not splitting hairs to insist upon certain differences between the hard-tempered age which produced the satires of Samuel Butler, the comedies of Wycherley, and Hobbes's *Leviathan*, and the later Augustan period— the England of Queen Anne and her immediate successors —with its increasing refinements of speech and sentiment. Swift was endowed with all the ruthlessly analytic energy which we see functioning in varied forms in the political-religious satire of *Hudibras* and the social satire of the Restoration comedies. Somewhere in the course of the seventeenth century men ceased to feel and think symbolic-ally—as Milton still did when in the youthful *Nativity Ode* he wrote of the music of the spheres and the angelic har-monies, thus symbolizing the universal order—and became rationalists. After all the contentions and animosities of the Civil War, the Restoration mind was on guard against the fantastic and the hypocritical. Truth could no longer be taken for granted: it had to be discovered amidst all manner of falsities and deceptions. It was natural that the exposure of hypocrisy should habitually pass into denial of the more general claims of sentiment. Samuel Butler had written in one of his prose *Characters* that no art can raise the mind of man higher than music. 'But,' he went on, 'it is but in a dream, and when the music is done, the mind wakes and comes to it self again.' This anti-romantic spirit, this refusal to admit the validity of anything save the bare and naked truth arrived at through rational analysis, Swift shares fully with the men of the Restoration.

The mind that dominated Restoration thought was Hobbes's. It dominated it not by winning assent but arousing such a wide-spread feeling of repulsion that philosophic writing of the period was as often as not direct refutation of the dangerous errors propounded by the author of the *Leviathan*. Swift was as ready as the rest to combat Hobbes and his materialism, though he admired him as a great and formidable antagonist. Indeed, there is an astringency in Swift which is close to that of Hobbes. Furthermore, each was in his own way a moralist, deeply concerned to understand the behaviour of man. Each began by stripping humanity of all pretensions. What was thus revealed constituted for Hobbes a point of departure lying within nature itself, and man's achievements—the ordered society, stability in the state—were won by acknowledging and implementing these fundamental drives of fear and desire. In contrast, Swift took the traditional view of what constituted 'natural' conduct. For him the Natural was that which was defined by perennial Reason and achieved through restraint and discipline. If the stripping operation revealed things as they are, it revealed them as they ought not to be. '*Reason* itself,' he once wrote, 'is true and just, but the *Reason* of every particular Man is weak and wavering, perpetually swayed and turned by his Interest, his Passions, and his Vices.' The divines of the Restoration period, while perfectly familiar with this kind of anti-rationalism—the indictment, by the moral rationalist, of man's habitually irrational conduct—came at the problem differently: the older among them through the concepts of sin, repentance, and Divine assistance; the younger, committed to answering Hobbesianism, by declaring that man was indeed actuated by feeling and passions but by feeling and passions of love and sympathy. It was moral doctrine of the latter sort which came to be thoroughly established in English thought and letters of the Augustan age—the doctrine of benevolence and its accompanying forms of sentimentalism. If Swift's relentless moral rigorism is to be understood it must be located historically in the earlier era. While essentially traditional and Christian, it was not as a rule expressed in the language of theology. Nor did it ever yield to the newer theories of human geniality: it remained as hard and in its way as harsh as anything in Hobbes.

Another context, quite as important as the one we have been speaking of, is to be found in certain characteristic features of Restoration Anglicanism. Swift's loyalty to the Established Church as an institution has never been questioned, though he has frequently been represented as a churchman in form rather than in spirit. A fuller knowledge of Swift on the one hand and Anglicanism on the other not only establishes his sincerity beyond doubt but reveals the extent to which many of his fundamental attitudes were those of the Church during his formative years. The *via media*—the middle way between Roman Catholicism and Puritan Dissent—was a concept dear to the Restoration clergy. Day after day, year after year they hammered away at it in their sermons: whereas Roman Catholicism rested in sheer faith and Puritan Dissent in sheer inspiration, the Established religion was able to justify itself through the voice of reason, and was in this sense a reasonable faith. But the defence of this middle position of theirs called for more than calm exposition of the 'grounds of the credibility' of their faith. Their enemies had to be kept under constant fire, with the result that anti-Catholicism and anti-Puritanism constituted a large and readily distinguishable element in Anglican sermons of the Restoration. The language used by Restoration divines in describing Roman Catholic and Puritan could be uncharitable, racy, sometimes unforgivably vulgar according to any modern standard. It has been said more than once that only a man who was at bottom indifferent to all religions could have written the *Tale of a Tub*, so coarse is the satire which Swift has there directed against both Catholicism and Dissent. As a matter of fact, the *Tale* is one of the notable expositions of the *via media*, and though its tone is more impertinent, its satiric language more cogent than what we find in the ordinary sermons of the time, there were preachers —Robert South comes to mind—who did not hesitate to use ridicule and acerbity.

Swift's unreserved acceptance of this doctrine of the middle way carried with it an entire complex of ideas, theories, perceptions, assumptions. Three of these may be mentioned: the interpretation of Puritanism as political tyranny; the analysis and rejection of enthusiasm; and the defence of matters of Christian faith against deistic criticism. In the view which represented the Puritan régime of the 1640s and '50s as political tyranny—tyranny being the seizure of power by a minority within the state—is to be found one important source of Swift's political ideas. He opposed any further concessions to the Dissenters of his time, holding that they now enjoyed religious toleration but ought under no circumstances to be admitted to positions within the government, national or local, lest they seize the power, as their ancestors had once done, and force the will of a minority upon the whole nation. This scarcely amounts to persecution of the Dissenters, but it does bring Swift within the spirit of what is sometimes called the persecuting Church of the Restoration. What can easily be left out of account in considering these matters is the presence of certain reasoned theories. The theory of the *via media* was one of these, closely argued, precisely defined. Another was a concept of rational liberty which Swift among others arrived at through the traditionally hostile view of Puritanism.

The Restoration era is notable for its rejection of 'enthusiasm'. The term was constantly in use, and though not confined to matters of religion was applied primarily to the kind of inspiration to which many of the lesser Puritan sects had, or were believed to have laid claim. The will of God did not thus declare itself. Faith derived from abnormal emotional experience carried no verifiable credentials. Again the *via media* was invoked, again the reasonable faith of the Anglican Church was insisted upon while the absurdities of religious enthusiasm were being exposed. It is readily apparent that rationalism of this order did not have to extend itself by much in order to chill a great deal more than the ardours of religion. Swift's suspicion of enthusiasm in all its forms is a case in point. It was something, this wide-ranging suspicion of his, which was given in the rational faith which made up such a large part of his world-view: the romantic, the imaginative flight carried us out of ourselves only to land us in the realm of nonsense.

Finally, the position which Swift took in his sermon *On the Trinity* (precise date unknown) accords perfectly with rational faith as defined by those who preached the *via media*. Faith is grounded in reason, but there *is* faith and there *are* limits to human reason. The doctrine of the Trinity is not in contradiction to but beyond reason; the Christian accepts it because it is revealed. The present historical approach has, it is hoped, made it clear that the contour of Swift's religious thought coincides with that of Restoration Anglicanism. Such thought is properly described as rational, but we must not overlook the restrictions which were still placed upon reason and human knowledge. Christianity was more than blind faith, but what was given through Revelation lay beyond the reach of any rational process. The argument against deism as presented by Swift and the rational divines of whom we have been speaking rests upon this emphatic delimitation of reason.

A third context—the first being that of Swift's moral rigorism, the second of his religious assumptions and their extension in various directions—may be identified in the doctrines of common sense. These doctrines were not peculiar to the Restoration era but were maintained down through the eighteenth century. In fact, it is their presence throughout the entire period bounded on one side by the Jacobeans and on the other by the romantics which leads us to speak of this century and a half as the period of the English Enlightenment. The belief in common sense was a belief in a particular sort of reason—not in this instance in the reason of the moralists, nor again in the reason of the rational divines, but in what amounted to the funded experience of mankind. In our 'common notions' lay a short cut both to truth and to every-day working principles. This trust in the reliability of the common notions is to be seen, however, as the consequence of more basic assumptions concerning the nature of man and human experience. The Enlightenment had created for itself—by placing new emphasis upon certain traditional elements of western thought —the image of the normal man, of normal human experience. The modern mind was as yet relatively untouched by any of those startlingly different concepts and values which, establishing themselves by the close of the eighteenth century, led the romantics to search for the significant in the unusual, sometimes the abnormal, and induced a general feeling that conformity meant intellectual and spiritual sterility. We must understand that in demanding conformity to the accepted patterns of thought and behaviour the Enlightenment was not attempting to suppress anything save what, under its principles, had every appearance of wayward foolishness. Man found himself by living in the common forms. On the side of social thought, Swift's age had more confidence in the fundamental sanity of man and in the natural health of society than is sometimes realized. It had not yet come upon the idea of progress but through its faith in common sense and all which that faith implied it was not without a certain cautious optimism. Swift himself, in his political writing, is constantly measuring the stupidity and malfeasance of individual politicians and public figures against the good sense and decency inherent in the social body. Here is an aspect which has often been overlooked, perhaps because Swift so fascinates us that we sometimes lose sight of his satiric norm. But we cannot genuinely understand him as a satirist until we perceive how often his sensationalism is devised to bring us back to common sense, to our common humanity. It is a sensationalism resulting not from despair but from a determination to assert the reasonable and the normal against all deviations.

Swift's anti-intellectualism is likewise to be seen in this same context. Modern science was founded in the seventeenth century, and by the eighteenth had firmly entrenched itself and was beginning to remould English thought and, through practical applications, to change the economic life of the English people. However, a certain predisposition against the new science is to be observed in the writings of the Augustan wits. Some of these, like Dr. Arbuthnot, were themselves scientists, and in many instances their ridicule was not directed at science as such but at the absurdities which could be committed in its name. One feels that Swift's thrusts at the scientists usually go further than this, but it should be observed that in most instances of this sort his satire has a very wide field of dispersion, taking in a great many forms of mistaken intellectual endeavour. Common sense again supplied the norm. Though our sympathy today is not likely to extend to the kind of anti-intellectualism which often resulted, an understanding of Swift's position and its correlations will at least enable us to draw up our indictment with reasonable accuracy.

In summarizing Swift's place in relation to the thought of his time we may say that he was a rationalist in three somewhat different senses: he believed that reason should govern our irrational instincts; in religion he embraced a rational faith, finding in the Anglican *via media* a position from which to attack Catholicism, tyrannical Puritanism, enthusiasm, and critical deism; he likewise lived and thought in terms of that reasonableness which, it was assumed, spoke through common sense and lay at the centre of all human experience conforming to the normal. This is not meant to imply that he was ever a philosopher in the strict sense. But in his age the articulate man, satirist no less than spokesman on political and religious affairs, was a man of ideas. Swift's mind moved readily among the currents of Restoration and eighteenth-century thought, sometimes with these currents, sometimes against them, and it is possible to follow the general course it took. In doing so we are not losing touch with the satiric artist. On the contrary. Among the preliminary questions properly presenting themselves to Swift's literary critics are such as concern his character as a man of the Enlightenment. His satiric statements are not grounded in the presuppositions of our own time nor of those of the nineteenth century. In temper and sensibility no less than in theories and ideas they are characteristic expressions of European and more specifically English culture of those years lying between the late Renaissance and the French Revolution. Swift's genius was not original but representative.

The most important aspect of Swift is the one just suggested, which presents itself when we consider the broad literary tradition within which he falls. His place is alongside of Samuel Butler, Pope, Goldsmith, Fielding, Jane Austen, for it is in such writers that the age of comic vision spoke most clearly. As Yeats would have said, their works thought in them. Themes, language, techniques were in a sense part of what they felt about the human situation which they assessed from much the same point of observation and always—with the exception of the later Fielding—in terms of comic perception. Theirs was not a vision of progress but of man's habitual involvement in ridiculous circumstances. Comedy, as they understood and practised it, was the means of recording the manifold ways in which the human race contrived to distort itself and generally to misconstrue its natural and proper functions and ends. But such a comic mode as this—hard-tempered, alive with energy, working often through grotesque representations— did not fare well in the presence of the new romantic spirit, the rise of which spelt the end of so much that had been characteristic of the Enlightenment. Men now ceased to be ridiculous and became instead unfortunate and frustrated, and the satirists on their part underwent a corresponding change and began to labour under a sense of guilt and of implication in some vast cosmic evil. Swift and the other writers of his age who were marked by the *vis comica* were utterly untouched by any such spirit as this. As satiric commentators they stood well apart from the scenes they depicted. In doing so and in allowing us to share with them this sense of distance they were defining—in the peculiar manner of artistic statement—the gap between the natural and the unnatural. We were to attain normality by guarding against pride, and this we could very well do by observing the distorted figures given in comedy. Of the many misapprehensions of Swift none is wider of the mark than that which represents him as a satirist who wrote out of a bitter mind and a bitter heart, who saw only man's ineptitude and failure, and who despised his fellows because he first despised himself. It is not love that Swift expresses, but neither is it hatred. His comic sense kept him, as it did the writers who belong with him, in a region lying between.

Swift's energy—more precisely, the kinetic quality of his satire—cannot well be accounted for unless he is regarded as a fully conscious artist, a literary craftsman using considered means to attain desired effects. Whatever term we give to Swift's period—the Enlightenment, the age of comic vision—we recognize that in literature it did not do its work with the assistance of that concept which served later generations and came to be called creative imagination. Swift and his fellows spoke of wit and invention ; when they used the word *imagination* they meant by it a psychological faculty which produced mental images, or if they used it more broadly, the mistaken visions of the enthusiast. But as artists it is no longer possible to maintain that in the usual sense of the word as it occurs in present-day criticism they were without artistic imagination. What Swift does with words is what the poet does, and his satiric devices are means whereby a view of man is given translation. Swift's intuition is more often than not expressed in negative terms —that, indeed, is the essence of his irony. But it is a 'positive' : the repudiation of the false, a clarified and clarifying sense of the realities of human experience, the faith that man is free so long as he asserts the tradition of reason against stupidity and bestiality.

III

THE SATIRIC ARTIST: INITIAL PHASE

THE *Tale of a Tub* was published anonymously in London in May 1704. It consisted of three parts, the *Tale* itself, the *Battle of the Books*, and the *Discourse Concerning the Mechanical Operation of the Spirit*. Swift had been in England since the previous November, and it is reasonable to suppose that the chief purpose behind his visit had been to arrange for the appearance of his first great satiric work, brought nearly to completion during his final residence at Moor Park. Whether his negotiations with the eventual publisher, John Nutt, were as complicated and secretive as suggested in the various notices purportedly inserted in the *Tale* by the bookseller, we may be certain that Swift took every possible means to ensure anonymity. By withholding his name—as he had likewise done three years before in the case of his effective political pamphlet, the *Contests and Dissensions in Athens and Rome*—he secured a certain amount of protection against immediate hostility. But it would seem that he had a further reason, more complex. Anonymity was not only part of the literary game which the wits had been playing since the Restoration, it was the all-important element, the basic stratagem, in the Swiftian comedy. In the *Tale* he nowhere appears *in propria persona*. Various people are made to address us—who they are will be discussed presently—but they are characters such as a dramatist brings upon the stage. The anonymity which Swift was officially to maintain throughout his career as a satiric writer is, in a most important sense, an aspect of his creative imagination.

But even if Swift had openly declared his authorship, there were few people to whom in 1704 his name would have meant anything. True, he had recently supervised the publication of four volumes of Temple's literary remains, and had identified himself as editor of these. But the *Contests and Dissensions* (1701), his sole claim to anything in the way of distinction, had appeared without any name, and though some of the influential Whigs seem to have learned who the author was, they might have had some difficulty in recognizing in the satirist one previously established in their minds as a judicious political commentator. Thus in effect the appearance of the *Tale* announced the presence among the writers of the period of a new and striking personality. Even today, despite the fact that we know a good deal more about Swift's youth and his early literary experiments than any of his contemporaries—his closest friends excepted—ever did, the *Tale* still surprises. It is as though a hitherto unknown satiric artist of brilliance and maturity were revealing himself for the first time. We can make out a certain resemblance to the author of the early poems, but the Swift who by 1696 was at work on the *Tale* was one who had undergone a startling transformation of literary personality—a transformation in everything having to do with imaginative point of view and distinctive idiom. In this respect Swift is unlike almost any other writer that comes to mind. With him it was not a matter of development but, so far as we can judge, of sudden discovery.

The poetry which Swift wrote in the early days at Moor Park, before he turned prose satirist, is of peculiar interest in that it shows us something of Swift's literary mind before it underwent the transformation we have been speaking of. But before taking up certain aspects of the verse which help us towards an understanding of the *Tale of a Tub*, let us run through some of the factual details concerning the three satiric compositions which made up the 1704 volume. First in both position and importance is the *Tale* itself, consisting of some sixteen quite separate parts, each bearing its own title or number. There are five prefatory sections : the bookseller's—i.e. the publisher's—*Dedication*, the book-seller's notice to the reader, an *Epistle Dedicatory*, a *Preface*, an *Introduction*. Of the eleven sections which follow, those setting forth the story of the three brothers, Peter, Martin, and Jack, are arranged alternately with the so-called *Digressions*. Swift himself was later to point out that the satirical materials of the *Tale* were drawn from 'the numerous and gross corruptions in religion and learn-ing,' and however much of the subtlety and informing comedy may escape the casual reader, he can scarcely fail to recognize that there are two such themes and that these are made to appear alternately, 'corruptions in religion' underlying the fable of the three brothers, 'corruptions in learning' supplying the matters treated in the *Digressions*. Furthermore, the allegory which is given in the story of the brothers is made completely obvious : Peter, Martin, and Jack represent, respectively, Roman Catholicism, the Church of England, and Dissent, and the strange behaviour of both Peter and Jack as against the common sense finally acquired by Martin is illustration of the Anglican *via media*.

In the second place, with its own title page, is the *Battle of the Books*. Described as a 'full and true account', it begins as historical narrative and ends as though it were an epic in prose. It differs from the *Tale* in being very much of an occasional satire, for one of Temple's essays had recently been subjected to sharp criticism, and Swift was seeking to defend his patron by casting ridicule upon the two writers responsible for this attack, William Wotton and Richard Bentley. His immediate purpose was supported, however, by a more general one : namely to present in an effective light the central position of the 'ancients' as this had come to be defined in the course of the so-called 'quarrel of the ancients and moderns'. This quarrel had been going on, in one form or another, throughout the seventeenth century, though France rather than England

had been the centre. Temple had become involved in it
through his essay *Upon the Ancient and Modern Learning*
(1690), in which he had set out to refute those who were
upholding as a matter of historical fact the superiority of
modern arts and civilization. Temple himself held to a
cyclic theory of history. He was thus unable to accept any
form of progressivism; and where the arts were concerned,
he was a 'man of taste' with a traditional preference for
classical over modern literature. All of this made him an
'ancient', as the phrase went, and fair game for any of the
'moderns' who chose to call him to account. William
Wotton was the first to challenge. He did so in a typical
'modern' manifesto, *Reflections upon Ancient and Modern
Learning* (1694). But it was the great philologist Richard
Bentley, then keeper of the Royal Library at St. James's
Palace, who dealt the sharpest blow. Temple, in attempting to establish the superiority of ancient prose literature,
had unfortunately cited Aesop's *Fables* and the *Epistles* of
Phalaris. In a *Dissertation* appended in 1697 to a new
edition of Wotton's *Reflections* Bentley cut the ground from
under Temple's feet by showing that the *Fables* and the
Epistles were both spurious. Though Swift indicated no
great interest in the specific details marking the dispute
between Temple and his two opponents, he resented what
all of Temple's friends insisted was the unmannerly behaviour of Wotton and Bentley. The 'moderns' as such
he regarded with profound contempt, classifying them as
merely another group of enthusiasts. On the theoretical
side he refused to be drawn into debate, but his position
is clear enough. It is simply this: excellence knows no
time. Swift viewed history substantively, in terms of out-
standing characters and achievements. Neither the progressivism of the moderns nor the cyclic theory of Temple
excited in him any curiosity or interest.

The last of the three satires, cast in the form of a Letter
to a Friend, is the *Discourse Concerning the Mechanical*

Operation of the Spirit. It consists of two sections, devoted respectively to religious zeal as experienced by Dissenters when at worship and as manifested by their 'Enthusiastic Preachers'.

Everything that we know about the composition of the three pieces seems to show that they were mostly written in the period between 1696 and 1699.[1] The *Tale* must have been substantially finished at the time of Temple's death early in 1699, though apparently Swift continued to retouch it down to the eve of publication, and two preliminary sections—the *Dedication to Somers* and the bookseller's notice to the reader—would seem to have been added in 1704. Two events which occurred in the quarrel involving Temple and his two chief opponents help to date the *Battle of the Books*: the immediate occasion of Swift's satire was Bentley's first *Dissertation*, and this was published in June 1697, while the episode which brings the *Battle* to a close refers to an anti-Bentley pamphlet appearing in March 1698. The *Mechanical Operation* reads very much like one of the *Digressions* in the *Tale* and is presumably of corresponding date.

Why Swift waited until the spring of 1704 to publish his satire we shall never know. He probably had good reason to withhold it while Temple was still alive, for Sir William is known to have disapproved of what he called 'ridicule', which he regarded as one of the corrupting forces in contemporary letters. But Temple's death gave him a clear field. In any event, the *Tale* did not come from the press until May 1704, and by 1 June Swift was back in

[1] Though there were stories to the effect that Swift had begun the allegory of the three brothers while still a student at Trinity College, it seems more likely that this part of the satire, which is apparently the earliest, dates in the form in which we now have it from 1696. Whether Swift was still at Kilroot at the time or had returned to Temple's house is not known. The *Digressions* have every appearance of being later than the sections containing the account of Peter, Martin, and Jack, and it is not believed that they were begun before the latter part of 1697.

Ireland. If his purpose had been to gain the attention of the world of letters, he was not long in realizing that he had indeed done just that. The *Tale* was a *succès de scandale*. It was attributed to Temple, to Lord Somers, to Smalridge. The latter, an eminent divine, indignantly denied that he was the author, and declared to a friend that not all they both possessed or ever should possess would have hired him to write it.[1] Before the year was out, a book had appeared expressly against it, describing it as 'a Tincture of . . . Filthiness'.[2] Atterbury, Swift's future friend, was more perceptive. He found it well written. He was also of the opinion—referring apparently to the satire against the Dissenters—that it would do good service. But he foresaw that the 'profane strokes' would be misrepresented and would work against the author's reputation and interest in the world.[3] And in 1705 William Wotton, who had been attacked in both the *Tale* and the *Battle*, secured his revenge by publishing his *Observations upon The Tale of a Tub* (appended to his *Defence of the Reflections upon Ancient and Modern Learning*), in which he gave it as his solemn judgement that this notorious satire was 'one of the Prophanest Banters upon the Religion of *Jesus Christ*, as such, that ever yet appeared'.

The sales of the book must have been considerable for two further editions were called for before the close of 1704 and the fourth edition appeared in 1705. By 1709, when Swift had gained a recognized place among the Whig men of letters, thanks largely to the Bickerstaff papers, he was generally acknowledged to be the author of the *Tale*, and a new edition of the satire seemed justified. It was for this that he wrote the *Apology*, which is dated 3 June 1709 and was inserted in the fifth edition of the *Tale*, which appeared

---

[1] See Johnson, 'Swift', in the *Lives of the Poets*.

[2] William King, *Some Remarks On The Tale of a Tub* (1704).

[3] Atterbury to Harley, 1704, Hist. Mss. Com., Portland, IV, 155.

late in 1710.[1] The *Apology* is the clearest sort of statement. Swift's chief purpose was, of course, to convince the too literal-minded that the work was not, as Wotton had expressed it, a profane banter upon Christianity, but rather a seriously motivated satire. It was here that he described his materials as having been furnished by 'the numerous and gross corruptions in religion and learning'. Altogether, Swift goes about as far as any writer can be expected to do in giving us helpful leads. He mentions Marvell's *Rehearsal Transpros'd*, perhaps as good a key as any to the methods employed in the *Tale*. He reminds us that in certain passages 'the author personates the style and manner of other writers'. He observes that wit is a noble gift and humour an agreeable one, the two combining to render any work acceptable to the world. Statements such as these have such an obvious appearance that at first they do not seem to be revealing very much. It is only after we have otherwise found our way into the *Tale* that we perceive their full import.

Of Swift's early poems, six have come down to us. First in point of time is the *Ode to the King*, written after Swift's return to Ireland in 1690. The others were composed at Moor Park during his second residence there, which lasted from December 1691 to the summer of 1694. Four are Pindaric *Odes* in the manner of Cowley, two are in decasyllabic couplets. They are curious compositions—scarcely poetry, perhaps, though marked now and then by powerfully rhythmic passages and imagery of an exact if too conceptual order. But if they are read at all today, it is as

---

[1] This fifth edition became the definitive one, and added still more complexities and further comedy to the satiric work: the *Apology* increased the number of sections in the *Tale* to seventeen; eight illustrations appeared here for the first time; and to the marginal notes of the first four editions Swift added two more sets, printed at the bottom of the page, the unsigned ones being probably his own, those bearing the name of Wotton having been coolly lifted from that writer's *Observations upon The Tale of a Tub*.

commentary upon the later Swift. What does his 'young and (almost) Virgin-muse'—described thus in the *Ode to the Athenian Society*—have to tell us about the making of the satiric artist?

The moral-intellectual orientation, we soon perceive, is not substantially different from what we have come to recognize as characteristic of Swift in his maturity. In the *Ode to the Athenian Society* we find the young poet attacking the wits and atheists of his day: they have taken over the stage and 'fain would rule the Pulpit'. In the closing stanza of this same poem he gives a picture of the final triumph of pedantry and pride as the 'Gothic Swarms' of ignorance descend upon the nations. In the *Ode to . . . Temple* he proceeds to build up a detailed contrast between his patron, with his civilized attitude towards the things of the mind, and the ill-mannered pedants who seek to purchase knowledge, which to them is merely a matter of memory, at the expense of good breeding and common sense. Sancroft, the Archbishop of Canterbury who as a non-juror had been deprived of his See in 1690, is praised, in the *Ode* addressed to him, for his firmness of purpose and for pointing out the way which leads to Christ, a way which a world of 'mistaken idiots' have wholly missed. It is here, too, that the 'wild reformers' of the Church are described as tearing Religion's face and stripping her of ornaments in their efforts 'to wash off th' imaginary paint'. In writing his lines to Congreve, on the occasion of the latter's second successful play, the poet returns to literary matters and pays his respects to the false critics of the theatre, who overrun the pit like 'swarms of gnats'.

Throughout all this verse the dominant manner is that of Juvenalian satire and the main themes concern evils, abuses, and shortcomings in the two areas of learning and religion. Indeed, if satire were wholly a matter of intellectual substance and moral judgements, the distance separating these poems and the *Tale of a Tub*, concerned as the latter is with 'the numerous and gross corruptions in religion and learning', would not be as great as we instantly recognize it to be. But the difference between the satire as we find it in the verses and what we have in the three prose pieces is a qualitative thing. Swift the poet is a very self-conscious and therefore self-centred writer. His manner of approach is direct, his pronouncements and denunciations all seem to have a very personal air. The *Tale*, on the other hand, has been worked out in an entirely different mode. It is dramatic—its idiom and controlling point of view are not those of Jonathan Swift but of characters—non-selves—created for purposes of ironic presentation.

A closer reading of these same poems would readily bring to light other details of phrasing and imagery which seem to anticipate the *Tale*. Further than that, it would show that Swift had already hit upon certain of the concepts or extended images that he was going to employ in different and greatly elaborated form in his later work. Take, for instance, the fourth and fifth stanzas of the *Ode to the Athenian Society*. Here the wits and atheists of the age are described as a 'hopeful Sect', having their own system or set of principles—which is to reduce everything to terms of sense—and characterized by certain materialistic beliefs in consequence of which they hold that all writing—by which they presumably mean words printed on paper—is merely a justling heap of atoms brought together not by men we call writers, not by human intelligence, but automatically and by eternal fate. We note, however, the seriousness—the indignant seriousness—of this description of sect and myth. It is witty only in that it is keenly analytical; humour, imaginative expansion, ironic verve are all lacking.

Swift recognized that his first attempts at verse were singularly unsuccessful and gave up in disgust. It was only after an interval of some five years, in the course of which he found his true vein in prose satire, that he ventured again to try the medium of verse. He was no longer an immature

writer when, perhaps in 1698, he composed the poem
entitled *Verses wrote in a Lady's Ivory Table-Book*. From
that moment on he was at home in verse of a kind which
answered in its fashion to the satiric idiom first established
in the *Tale of a Tub*. To say that Swift was never a great
poet is not putting it in quite the right way. He was not,
of course—we do not have to go outside the eighteenth-
century frame of reference to assure ourselves not only of
his inferiority to many other poets but to himself as a prose
writer. None the less, his full acknowledgement of his own
lesser talent, his willingness to stay within certain self-
imposed and clearly understood limits, and the jauntiness
and energy with which he went about his business give
him a more clearly defined place among minor English
poets than many have realized. We may learn a good deal
from *Verses wrote in a Lady's Ivory Table-Book*, an early
poem, if not the earliest, in Swift's new manner:

> Peruse my Leaves thro' ev'ry Part,
> And think thou seest my owners Heart,
> Scrawl'd o'er with Trifles thus, and quite
> As hard, as senseless, and as light:
> Expos'd to every Coxcomb's Eyes,
> But hid with Caution from the Wise.
> Here you may read (*Dear Charming Saint*)
> Beneath (*A new Receit for Paint*)
> Here in Beau-spelling (*tru tel deth*)
> There in her own (*far an el breth*)
> Here (*lovely Nymph pronounce my doom*)
> There (*A safe way to use Perfume*)
> Here, a Page fill'd with Billet Doux;
> On t'other side (*laid out for Shoes*)
> (*Madam, I dye without your Grace*)
> (Item, *for half a Yard of Lace*.)
> Who that had Wit would place it here,
> For every Peeping Fop to Jear.
> To think that your Brains Issue is
> Expos'd to th' Excrement of his,

In power of Spittle and a Clout
When e're he please to blot it out;
And then to heighten the Disgrace
Clap his own Nonsense in the place.
Whoe're expects to hold his part
In such a Book and such a Heart,
If he be Wealthy and a Fool
Is in all Points the fittest Tool,
Of whom it may be justly said,
He's a Gold Pencil tipt with Lead.

The octosyllabic couplet was Samuel Butler's favourite form, and the fact that it also became Swift's tells us something about the sources of the latter's style and craftsmanship in verse. However, the effect which Swift has achieved in the *Lady's Ivory Table-Book* owes nothing to humorous double rhymes, which were Butler's forte, but on the other hand a great deal to conciseness of form and a certain epigrammatic quality. The piece is exactly as long as it needs to be, and though one can break it down into two rhetorical halves it is still a unit by virtue of its self-enclosing shape and its assured rhythmic movement. As social verse it takes us into a world already familiar to us from the Restoration comedy of manners, and displays this world from very much the same point of observation. Swift's approach to the basic incongruities which here constitute his satiric theme is two-fold. He compounds the incongruities, arranges them absurdly side by side, forces them into grotesque couplings. In this respect he has anticipated what Pope has done in the *Rape of the Lock* at greater length and with greater comic logic and charm. The other approach is the analytical one. *Strip* was a favourite word with Restoration writers and they used it in an almost symbolic sense, for theirs was a social comedy which gained its end by exposing our moral incongruities violently and in gross physical terms. Swift was to become the great master of what we might call the comedy of discontinuity: things are *not* the same —

clear through; when the surface is broken open, when the outer layer is peeled off, when the beau is stripped of his fine clothes, when the woman is flayed, we are impressed to find that the inside differs so curiously from the outside. The *Lady's Ivory Table-Book* is the earliest of a whole group of poems in which Swift sets some observer loose in a woman's dressing-room to make the closest of observations and to render a point by point account of his curious findings. Psychiatric explanations of the motivation involved here would be all very well if they did not leave Swift's purposes as writer quite out of account. The explorer in the dressing-room is a dramatization of the inside-outside contrast, and the nature of his discoveries accords perfectly with a comedy that characteristically works through images of nakedness and the functions of the human body.

To come, now, to the satiric craftsmanship of the *Tale of a Tub*. Our ultimate judgement of Swift may properly be more a moral than an artistic one, more concerned with his view of man and the quality of his intuition than with his precise methods as a writer. One's chief justification for examining his craftsmanship with some care is that it has so frequently been overlooked altogether or hurriedly passed over on the assumption that a satiric work of art is somehow no different from the satirist's broad intentions as a commentator on the human scene. A satire is as much a work of the literary imagination as is a poem or a drama. Its total effect—as distinct from what we sometimes think of as its 'purpose'—lies in its chosen language and imagery, while the point of view from which it is being delivered, the episodes themselves, the patterns in which the materia has been arranged are all in a sense contrived. Swift and the major writers of his age were, we may say, formalists that is they accepted the literary forms given them, they sometimes devised new ones of their own, but they alway worked through some form or other which they had sensed as such and whose possibilities they had calculated

Gulliver's Travels is a travel book; it is an imaginary voyage, a parody of a travel book; it is a take-off on the imaginary voyage—a parody of a parody. To see it in some such way and to watch Swift at work as he manipulates his extraordinarily complicated set of mirrors is not to lose sight of the perennial qualities of this greatest of all satiric Utopias or of Swift's guiding intuition. The *Tale of a Tub* has never enjoyed the popularity of the *Travels*, and there are students of Swift who are ready to fall in with the opinion held by most general readers that it is inferior to the latter both in what it sets out to do and in the way it closes upon its objective. Yet it remains the indispensable introduction to Swift's art. This is his satiric language, this the world as refracted in his comic imagination.

We may begin by asking ourselves how the three sections included in every edition of the work are supposed to stand in relation to one another. Are the *Tale*, the *Battle*, and the *Mechanical Operation* quite independent pieces which happen to have been printed together in the same volume, or do we have as it were a single satiric composition in three movements? It is likely that we are intended to ask precisely such questions, and to feel while asking them that it is impertinence on the part of the publisher, the author, or perhaps merely of the three satires lying in engaging juxtaposition that we should be forced to do so. Whatever our answers, we know of course that there is a certain unity of theme involved, all three satires deriving their materials from 'corruptions in religion and learning'. But what really establishes them as closely articulated members is the similarity in method of presentation. There is throughout the same order of invention, of imagery. Who is it that is addressing us? It is not Swift, save possibly in the very first fragment of all, the *Apology*, and even this is written impersonally with Swift—if it *is* Swift—appearing merely as 'the author'. As for the rest of the *Tale of a Tub* proper, it is the work, we discover, of several hands, we are not at first quite sure how many. It is 'the bookseller' who signs the *Dedication to Somers*—in the fifth edition this follows the *Apology* and thus becomes the second section—and who is supposedly the author of the section immediately following, *The Bookseller to the Reader*. With the fourth section, *The Epistle Dedicatory to Prince Posterity*, a quite different writer takes over. He is an enthusiastic 'modern', spokesman for the entire society of modern writers and defender of their works against all disparaging criticism, and he tells us that he is planning to vindicate his brethren at greater length in a treatise to be entitled a *Character of the present Set of Wits in this Island*. It is he who is speaking in all those sections of the *Tale* concerned with the follies of the learned—in the *Preface*, the *Introduction*, and the subsequent *Digressions*. It is he who is constantly calling to our attention the further treatises which he has written and which are to be speedily published. These are the treatises listed directly after the title-page and there announced as having all been written by the 'same author', i.e. the author of the *Tale*. What of the story of the three brothers? At first we are not aware that their history is being given us by a definite narrator, but as the story unfolds a speaker begins to materialize. 'I hope,' he writes, 'when this Treatise of mine shall be translated into Foreign Languages . . . that the worthy Members of the several *Academies* abroad . . . will favourably accept these humble Offers, for the Advancement of Universal Knowledge.' Further on, he promises not to forget his 'Character of an Historian', and at about the same time he confesses to a short memory, 'a Deficiency to which a true *Modern* cannot but of Necessity be a little subject'. Upon consulting the list of treatises standing at the head of the volume we learn that our historian is, after all, none other than the modern author whose acquaintance we have made in the *Digressions*. Thus the account of Peter, Martin, and Jack turns out to be another modern treatise,

So far Swift seems to have brought five personalities into play: the one who is writing the *Apology*, 'the author' referred to therein, 'the bookseller', the modern author, and the latter's *alter ego*, the historian. But there is still another, a sixth character, who appears on the stage only briefly but without whom the others would lose their meaning in the satiric comedy being enacted. This sixth character is not Swift, but he is a satirist—perhaps we should say, he is *the* satirist. Swift's irony depends upon our recognizing that the sentiments being expressed with such conviction are nonsense and that the characters who are delivering them are so frequently the opposite of all they profess to be, and in the hubbub of voices we must be aware of the voice of reason. The play otherwise ceases to be comedy. Whether Swift is always successful, whether he always wished to be successful, in establishing the presence of a satirist who acts as master of ceremonies we shall have to consider presently. In the *Tale* this impresario appears in the opening paragraphs of the *Preface*, and having told us how he has come to be selected as the one to devise this temporary expedient—the *Tale* itself—for diverting the attention of the wits of the present age, he proceeds to transform himself before our eyes into that modern writer whose voice we are to hear from this point forward.

The *Battle of the Books* and the *Mechanical Operation of the Spirit* are not greatly different in method. In the former there are three characters who address us: bookseller, author, and the historian—he assures us of his impartiality —who is giving the account of the battle between the books in the royal library. In the *Mechanical Operation* our old friend the bookseller writes a short advertisement, after which comes the *Discourse* itself, cast in the form of a Letter to a Friend, the author being a modern who describes himself as one who has always calculated his writings 'for universal Nature, and Mankind in General'. Do we have in historian and modern writer two new characters, or have

E

the figures from a *Tale of a Tub* made their reappearance?
The fact that we must ask such questions is the important
thing. That, indeed, is the important thing throughout.
We are never allowed to settle back in the assurance that
we know exactly where we are and what is scheduled to
— happen. The ground is always shifting under our feet and
we have to work to keep our balance. The tensions created
in this way not only arouse and sustain our interest but
communicate to us a sense of peculiar energy.

To become aware of the presence of these different characters is to prepare ourselves to follow what is taking place
on the stage. When the play is in actual progress we cannot choose in what order the acts shall appear, but in
analysis we are permitted to begin with the shorter second
and third acts—the *Battle* and the *Mechanical Operation*—
and leave until the last the very long and complicated *Tale*,
which comprises Act I. The *Battle of the Books* is a story
narrated, as we have seen, by one who describes himself
as 'being possessed of all Qualifications requisite in an *Historian*' and retained by neither of the two warring parties.
This claim to impartiality is perhaps borne out by the
reportorial tone of many of the episodes, but our historian's
true contempt for the moderns is too often reflected in his
choice of words for us to be deceived as to his real feelings.
But the *Battle* is not so much at the mercy of its central
speaker as are the two other pieces. The reason for this
lies in the fact that it is not an ordinary historical account
at all but an extended allegory in the form of an epic fragment: its episodes and the terms in which these episodes
are dealt with—chiefly, the kind of language and imagery
brought into play—are determined by the conditions of
allegory and epic. The opening passages of the *Battle* constitute an introduction. Next comes the episode of the bee,
the spider, and Aesop—a brilliant allegory within the larger
allegory that is the whole *Battle*. This is followed by the
description of Momus, patron deity of the moderns, his

journey to the den of Criticism, and the latter's progress from her native mountain in Nova Zembla to England, where she prepares to assist her son, William Wotton. The Goddess is described in these words:

[She] had Claws like a Cat: Her Head, and Ears, and Voice, resembled those of an *Ass*; Her Teeth fallen out before; Her Eyes turned inward, as if she lookt only upon herself: Her Diet was overflowing of her own *Gall*: Her *Spleen* was so large, as to stand prominent like a Dug of the first Rate, nor wanted Excrescencies in the form of Teats, at which a Crew of ugly Monsters were greedily sucking; and, what is wonderful to conceive, the bulk of Spleen encreased faster than the Sucking could diminish it.

Here we can forget the presence of the speaker and focus our attention upon the repulsive picture which has been drawn. The rest of the *Battle* is all a running account of important episodes occurring as the two armies engage one another, but there is a sharp alteration in tone as we come to the last encounter to be described, which finds Wotton and Bentley paired off against Temple and Boyle. Here the epic becomes the broadest of burlesques:

As when two *Mungrel-Curs*, whom *native Greediness*, and *domestick Want*, provoke, and join in Partnership, though fearful, nightly to invade the Folds of some rich Grazier; They, with Tails depress'd, and lolling Tongues, creep soft and slow . . .

The account breaks off at a fitting moment after giving us the image of Bentley and Wotton neatly skewered on Boyle's lance like a brace of woodcocks.

The positive elements in the *Battle of the Books* are unmistakable: the pedantry and ill manners of Wotton and Bentley, the shortcomings of the moderns, the sweetness and light of a culture that is neither old nor modern but perennial. Since the occasion of the satire was a dispute over literary matters it is fitting enough that the *Battle* should be cast in the best-known of all literary forms, the epic, and that the order of its language should be that derived directly or by way of parody from epic poetry.

If the *Mechanical Operation of the Spirit* is seen as an after-piece its farcical nature strikes us immediately. It is satiric *bravura*, fast paced, ironic from start to finish. Its irony is, however, of a peculiar sort which can perhaps be described as three-dimensional in contrast with the normal two-dimensional variety. In the latter what is said is directly opposite to what is meant, whereas the statement that Swift has devised for this occasion is not upside-down at all : it 'says what is meant' in the sense of arriving at a perfectly sound conclusion, but is totally wrong in its premises and all its reasoning. The intellectual comedy lies in the fact that the chief character, the writer of this Letter to a Friend, is a thorough-going modern who accepts modern material-ism *in toto* and is ready with evidence to prove that such things as poetry, eloquence, and politics are the result of processes which never involve anything beyond the nerves of the body and the senses. Using this mode of approach he proceeds to show that religious enthusiasm, fanaticism, and the art of canting or droning—i.e. preaching in the manner of the enthusiasts—are all mechanistic operations. Enthusiasm is declared to have its origin in the 'corruption of sense'. We in the audience have never, of course, believed otherwise, but it is a novel and diverting experience to sit by as the physical basis of a religious enthusiasm which we heartily contemn is being exposed by one who believes in nothing but the physical. The paradoxes which emerge as this skit unfolds were not intended, one believes, to bewilder and confuse, to make us doubt our own convic-tions and principles, but to draw from us an understanding response in the form of raucous laughter. There is an Aristophanic touch throughout. But if by chance we fail to see precisely what is taking place no great harm has been done, for we shall find ourselves in earnest agreement with the conclusion 'that the Seed or Principle, which has ever put Men upon *Visions* in Things *Invisible*, is of a

Corporeal Nature'. Failure to see in the author of the Letter a modern virtuoso who is a materialist in philosophy and who, in a manner parodying the deists', is searching for universal practices and beliefs—since practices and beliefs become true when shown to be universal—is to miss most of the comedy but not the positive doctrines to which Swift the man, Swift as a satirist, and his readers subscribe quite seriously.

By all odds the best comedy in this entertainment in three parts comes in the opening piece, the *Tale of a Tub*, the longest of the sketches, the most brilliant in conception, the most elaborately devised. Not only is impersonation as a method here carried to the limits of complication, but the workmanship from beginning to end displays the highest degree of ingenuity. In these respects the *Tale* is probably too ingenious, and its repeated failure—in Swift's own day and ever since—to exhibit its true satiric intentions immediately and unmistakably can in large part be attributed to its excessive cleverness of invention. On the other hand, we must recognize that it was never designed as an 'open' statement. Its spirit is that of a comedy of manners addressed to a small and very special audience. It is esoteric by intention, and because it is not compelled to expand its meaning and turn the highly charged phrase into a long commonplace it achieves a certain effect not otherwise to be come by. The style and imagery, under the control of parody and impersonation, are of a high order of wit—sometimes, indeed, of the order of poetry or of the next thing to it, intentional anti-poetry. Its action, its representations are genuine imaginative creations. And when, in its central section, the *Digression on Madness*, it pronounces judgement on the human enterprise in general and in doing so renders a further judgement, on life itself, it attains to a level which only comedy in its greatest moments ever reaches.

The *Tale* is so many different things all at once, it is moving round so many different axes, that description from a single point of reference is impossible. For one thing it pretends to be—all of it—an example of modern writing, and in the *Epistle Dedicatory* is described by its author as 'a faithful Abstract drawn from the Universal Body of all Arts and Sciences'. The modern men of letters with whom it is concerned, whose works it praises and summarizes, and whose various styles it sets out to imitate range from Dryden on the one hand to Wotton and Bentley on the other, with Tate, Durfey, Rymer, and Dennis falling in between. As a survey of modern wit and learning it takes in, before it has finished, the activities of Grub-Street (home of mean writers), Gresham College (meeting place of the Royal Society), Will's Coffee-house (resort of poets and critics), Warwick-Lane (where the Royal College of Physicians was located), Moorfields (Bedlam), and Westminster-Hall (symbol of the law). By its inclusion of the story of the three brothers it extends itself from the world of learning into that of religion as well, giving us an allegorical account of the break with Rome, the establishment of Anglicanism, and the subsequent conflicts between the Church of England and Dissent, and giving us this in the form of a narrative, modern in setting and tone, concerned with the 'progress' of three young men who come up to town and resolve to live according to the latest dictates of fashion.

Its form has already been discussed. There are seventeen separate sections, and these are supposedly the work of different writers: the person composing the *Apology*; the bookseller; the modern writer, author of the *Digressions*; and the historian who gives the account of the three brothers, and who turns out to be the modern writer. In addition to these characters, of whom the last two are of major importance, we have 'the author' as referred to in the *Apology* and, finally, someone who only appears for a few moments in the *Preface* but whose presence is felt throughout everything that ensues—the satirist who is presiding over the

entire sequence of comic scenes. Were it not for the occasional interjection of the latter's voice we should sometimes
—as in the *Digression on Madness*—lose track of the irony.

A work of art, it was generally agreed throughout the
Enlightenment, was properly an imitation of nature, a representation of the normal in the world outside us or in the
world of our own human experience. But the unnatural,
the grotesque, the humorous—i.e. something asquint—
were not thereby ruled out. Swift inherited from his pre-
decessors something in the way of a rhetorical theory
regarding grotesque art and its legitimate function. Samuel
Butler had recorded in his commonplace-book—though
there is no proof that Swift ever saw this—that wit 'delivers
things otherwise than they are in nature', employing 'those
things which it borrows of falshood to the benefit and
advantage of truth.' What was in a measure true of imaginative writing in general, by virtue of the fact that all such
writing worked through figurative language and hence distorted actuality, held doubly true of *genres* embodying satire,
comedy, the ridiculous, the ugly. These latter forms of
literature likewise served truth, but through depicting the
abnormal and doing so in a manner that further distorted
through comic exaggeration. The *Tale of a Tub* is not an
imitation of nature but of the grotesque and the unnatural,
which it brings before us in a number of ways that contri-
bute to an effect of superabundant energy. There are all
sorts of groups, each happy in its own identifying characteristics : modern writers, fashionable wits, the sect that worship the image of the tailor, the aeolists, dark authors,
critics, madmen, the brethren of Grub-Street, the wits of
Will's, the virtuosi of Gresham College. There are individual figures like Peter and Jack and the modern writer
whom we are engaged in reading. There are the beliefs
and enthusiasms peculiar to the different groups : the
beliefs entertained by the moderns, the theory that holds
that the universe is a suit of clothes and sees in the faculties

of the mind so many different forms of dress, the beliefs peculiar to the aeolists, to those defining happiness as credulity, to Peter the Roman Catholic, to Jack the Dissenter, and the humours of the present writer, his admiration for all that is modern, his love of dissection, the pride he takes in calling to our attention his further treatises, his passion for Prefaces, Epistles, Dedications, Digressions. There are projects, devices, systems at every turn : the *Tale of a Tub* is itself a device ; in the Preface we are told of an intended Academy for wits and of the schools it is to include.; Peter has his 'famous Discoveries, Projects, and Machines' ; the writer gives us, in his *Digression in the Modern Kind*, a recipe 'for a universal System in a small portable Volume, of all Things that are to be Known, or Believed, or Imagined, or Practised in Life' ; and the entire *Digression on Madness* is a project for the more effective use of madness in the commonwealth. There are 'types and fables' in the modern manner, the 'type' or symbolic representation being exemplified in the *Tale of a Tub* itself and the edifices in the air, the fable or allegory in the story of the three brothers. There are discourses or essays such as might have come from the pen of any one of a number of contemporary writers, including Dryden : an essay on imagination and invention, and another on satire, both in the *Preface* ; an essay on madness in the *Digression* devoted thereto ; and the essay which occurs in the *Mechanical Operation* and purports to explain the origin of poetry, eloquence, and political writing.

Here is Folly's plenty. But the exuberance lies not only in the apparently exhaustless varieties of senselessness which Swift's invention has provided but in the nature of the satiric drama itself. The *Tale* is really made up of a series of situations, in each of which some particular form of irrationality is expending its full energy in self-realization. It is as though we were being given to understand how Folly confers a special blessing upon each of the societies

existing to do her honour, how each has its own distin-
guishing enthusiasm, its own flight of fancy, system of
beliefs, and favourite projects and devices. Though Truth
is purely conceptual, and the life of reason is to be pursued without the aid of symbol and coloured vision, we
may allow Folly's children their sport, even going so far as to
encourage them in their enthusiasms and imaginative play.

The prose style, or more properly the styles exhibited
by the *Tale* are part of the drama of which we have just
been speaking. The question is whether we can anywhere
detect in this *mélange* of stylistic parodies a tone and manner
which are other than ironic. Such obviously are not present
in a passage like the following :

. . . the greatest Main given to that general Reception, which the
Writings of our Society have formerly received, (next to the transitory
State of all sublunary Things,) hath been a superficial Vein among
many Readers of the present Age, who will by no means be persuaded to inspect beyond the Surface and the Rind of Things;
whereas, *Wisdom* is a *Fox*, who after long hunting, will at last cost
you the Pains to dig out: 'Tis a *Cheese*, which by how much the
richer, has the thicker, the homelier, and the courser Coat; and
whereof to a judicious Palate, the *Maggots* are the best. 'Tis a *Sack-
Posset*, wherein the deeper you go, you will find it the sweeter.
Wisdom is a *Hen*, whose *Cackling* we must value and consider, because
it is attended with an *Egg*; But then, lastly, 'tis a *Nut*, which unless
you chuse with Judgment, may cost you a Tooth, and pay you with
nothing but a *Worm*.

This is a highly figurative style—'imaginative' in the strict
sense—but the imagery belongs entirely to the modern
author who is supposed to be writing at this point—the
passage is from the *Introduction*—and who has just told us
of his adoption into 'that Illustrious Fraternity' of Grub-
Street. But a somewhat different set of circumstances sur-
rounds the following, which occurs in the section describing
the aeolists.[1]

[1] Section VIII.

. . . whereas the mind of Man, when he gives the Spur and Bridle
to his Thoughts, doth never stop, but naturally sallies out into both
extreams of High and Low, of Good and Evil; His first Flight of
Fancy, commonly transports Him to Idea's of what is most Perfect,
finished, and exalted; till having soared out of his own Reach and
Sight, not well perceiving how near the Frontiers of Height and
Depth, border upon each other; With the same Course and Wing,
he falls down plum into the lowest Bottom of Things; like one who
travels the *East* into the *West*; or like a strait Line drawn by its
own Length into a Circle. Whether a Tincture of Malice in our
Natures, makes us fond of furnishing every bright Idea with its
Reverse; Or, whether Reason reflecting upon the Sum of Things,
can, like the Sun, serve only to enlighten one half of the Globe,
leaving the other half, by Necessity, under Shade and Darkness: Or,
whether Fancy, flying up to the imagination of what is Highest and
Best, becomes over-short, and spent, and weary, and suddenly falls
like a dead Bird of Paradise, to the Ground. Or, whether after all
these *Metaphysical* Conjectures, I have not entirely missed the true
Reason; The Proposition, however, which hath stood me in so much
Circumstance, is altogether true; That, as the most unciviliz'd Parts
of Mankind, have some way or other, climbed up into the Conception of a *God*, or Supream Power, so they have seldom forgot to
provide their Fears with certain ghastly Notions, which instead of
better, have served them pretty tolerably for a *Devil*.

Is this to be taken as another example of modern writing?
The phrase 'all these *Metaphysical* Conjectures' assures us
that the element of parody, of wryness, is by no means
absent, yet in effect the tone and the language which we
have here come pretty close to being those of the person
whom we have been referring to as the satirist. We feel,
as we do at certain moments in the *Digression on Madness*,
that we have proceeded beyond the irony and are close to
the dead centre of our Swiftian comedy.

We are to observe, finally, how two dominant motifs
run through the *Tale*, and how their development in opposition to one another forms the basic compositional pattern.
We are driven back and forth between two modes of

experience : creation, imaginative construction, the wild flight of fancy ; dissection, analysis. In symbolic terms the contrast is between the outside and the inside, between clothes and ornaments on the one hand and on the other the flayed woman, the dissected beau. Logically, it is the opposition of madness—unreason—and reason. But the *Tale* is an imaginative statement—one uses the term in its modern sense—and must deliver its meaning in its own peculiar language. One of the greatest passages in all satiric literature is that which comes in the middle of the *Digression on Madness*. The irony is complex, but to anyone who has been following the comedy up to this point it can scarcely be confusing. The modern writer is holding forth. But we are conscious that the satirist is standing close behind him, and the double system of references thus established leads us through the irony. Then, at the final semicolon, there is a dramatic change of tone and for a flash it is the satirist whose voice we hear. We are again at dead centre.

In the Proportion that Credulity is a more peaceful Possession of the Mind, than Curiosity, so far preferable is that Wisdom, which converses about the Surface, to that pretended Philosophy which enters into the Depth of Things, and then comes gravely back with Informations and Discourses, that in the inside they are good for nothing. The two Senses, to which all Objects first address themselves, are the Sight and the Touch ; These never examine farther than the Colour, the Shape, the Size, and whatever other Qualities dwell, or are drawn by Art upon the Outward of Bodies ; and then comes Reason officiously, with Tools for cutting, and opening, and mangling, and piercing, offering to demonstrate, that they are not of the same consistence quite thro'. Now, I take all this to be the last Degree of perverting Nature ; one of whose Eternal Laws it is, to put her best Furniture forward. And therefore, in order to save the Changes of all such expensive Anatomy for the Time to come ; I do here think fit to inform the Reader, that in such Conclusions as these, Reason is certainly in the Right ; and that in most Corporeal Beings, which have fallen under my Cognizance, the *Outside* hath been infinitely preferable to the *In* : Whereof I have been farther convinced from some late Experiments. Last Week I saw a Woman *flay'd*, and you will hardly believe, how much it altered her Person for the worse. Yesterday I ordered the Carcass of a *Beau* to be stript in my Presence; when we were all amazed to find so many unsuspected Faults under one Suit of Cloaths: Then I laid open his *Brain*, his *Heart*, and his *Spleen*; But, I plainly perceived at every Operation, that the farther we proceeded, we found the Defects encrease upon us in Number and Bulk: from all which, I justly formed this Conclusion to my self; That whatever Philosopher or Projector can find out an Art to sodder and patch up the Flaws and Imperfections of Nature, will deserve much better of Mankind, and teach us a more useful Science, than that so much in present Esteem, of widening and exposing them (like him who held *Anatomy* to be the ultimate End of *Physick*.) And he, whose Fortunes and Dispositions have placed him a convenient Station to enjoy the Fruits of this noble Art; He that can with *Epicurus* content his Ideas with the *Films* and *Images* that fly off upon his Senses from the *Superficies* of Things; such a Man truly wise, creams off Nature, leaving the Sower and the Dregs, for Philosophy and Reason to lap up. This is the sublime and refined Point of Felicity, called, *the Possession of being well deceived*; The Serene Peaceful State of being a Fool among Knaves.

IV

WHIG MAN OF LETTERS

AT the time of Temple's death early in 1699 Swift was thirty-one; upon his arrival in London in September 1710 at the outset of his career as a Tory publicist he was almost forty-three. The intervening twelve years constituted, as we have seen, a fairly well-defined period in his life. Though now vicar of Laracor, he made four visits to England, and there he gradually acquired something of a reputation both as a wit and as a writer on public affairs. His first pamphlet, *A Discourse of the Contests and Dissensions in Athens and Rome; with the Consequences they had upon both those States,* appeared in 1701 during the excitement occasioned by the impeachment of the Whig Lords by the Tory House of Commons. It was an effective piece of political writing, done entirely from the Whig point of view, and brought Swift—whose authorship came to be known—to the attention of Lord Somers and other Whig leaders. He was slow to follow up this initial success of his, but during the last of these four visits to England—it was the longest of them all, extending from November 1707 through June 1709— he turned again to public writing, though only two of the pamphlets which he then had in hand were published at this time (*A Letter Concerning the Sacramental Test*, December 1708; *A Project for the Advancement of Religion*, early 1709). In the meantime, as a result of the *Tale of a Tub*, now generally attributed to him, his friendship with Addison and Steele, and the leading *rôle* which he had taken in the Partridge hoax he had also come to be known as one of the wits of the period. Thus far, as matters had turned out, his associations had been with the Whigs, in the world of letters no less than in that of politics.

Throughout this period Swift made no secret of the fact that he was seeking his own advancement in the Church and that he hoped to secure this advancement through the favour of powerful Whigs like Somers, to whose aid he had come in the *Contests and Dissensions* and to whom the *Tale of a Tub* had been dedicated. But it was not long before he found himself in the midst of a drama of contemporary ideas and theories of a conflicting nature. In promoting his own private interests he was resolved never to act against his religious and political principles. But what, precisely, were these principles? Or rather, since he had always known where he stood on specific points, what pattern did they fall into, what line of procedure did they call for in the face of immediate situations arising out of the constant struggle for power now going on between the Whigs and Tories? Had he been content to remain quietly at home in Ireland and write his commentaries on politics and religion from that distance there would have been no problem at all. He would have had merely to put forward all his firm convictions, in which case he would have said what practically everyone of his class in Ireland believed, would have offended few who really mattered, and accomplished nothing at all. He had, however, chosen to follow a different course. His repeated visits to London kept him abreast of contemporary affairs. When he wrote, sensing his power to bring words to bear on events, he did so always with some clear and immediate purpose in view. And stating one's convictions on religious and political subjects now meant, as much as anything, taking up a resolute position regarding the Church-State relationship.

Behind the open conflicts marking so much of the seventeenth century there had lain a number of opposing theories concerning the relations between Church and State. Despite the fact that the Revolution of 1688 had resolved many long-standing questions, it had not offered a universally acceptable solution of this problem of the respective grounds and powers of secular government and Established Church. From 1660 on into the reign of James II the Anglican clergy had generally embraced the doctrine of passive obedience to the sovereign, but what they essentially had had in mind was the mutual dependence of Church and King upon one another. With the departure of James, the coming of William and Mary, and the refusal of the non-jurors to acknowledge either the new sovereigns or the dependence of the Church upon a *de facto* government, the entire question of Church-State relationship was brought into the open once more. The non-jurors had the force of logic with them, but their complete withdrawal from the active world was scarcely a practical answer. The Tories, by reason of their High-Church sympathies, were hostile to all movements designed to broaden the Church for the accommodation of the Dissenters and were disposed to uphold the theory of the Church's independence of state control. However, they could scarcely go against recent events, which had demonstrated the Church's dependence upon the secular powers, without calling the Revolution itself in question and thus retreating in political theory to the old doctrine of the absolute royal prerogative, and this they had no desire to do in these first years of the new century. The Whigs, on the other hand, were Erastian by tradition, opposed to all theories representing the Church as autonomous, and it remained to be seen how far they were willing to go in support of the Established Church at the expense of the Nonconformists, who had always been their natural political allies.

There was at no time any doubt in Swift's mind where he himself stood on all the points at issue here. He was Anglo-Irish, a protégé of Sir William Temple, and an ardent Churchman, and in each of these respects he had acquired certain very decided views. The Anglo-Irish colony, in the midst of which he had grown up, had been

Whig by necessity, and only recently had been rescued from mortal danger by King William, who had been forced to undertake his military campaign in Ireland because of the revolt of the native population during the months following upon the Revolution in England. To Swift and all those of his class in Ireland the cause of the Stuarts never ceased to mean aid and comfort to the enemy at home. At Moor Park Swift had had a thorough grounding in the political principles of his patron, which, as in the essay *Upon the Original and Nature of Government* (1679), were altogether in the liberal tradition. In his churchmanship Swift again reflected his Irish background. It is difficult to believe that he could ever, under any circumstances, have relented towards the Dissenters, whom he never ceased to think of as the direct inheritors of a tradition of fanaticism, rebellion, and tyranny, but the fear in which he held them was the immediate result of conditions in Ireland, where they made up a majority of the Protestants, and his firm determination to see them forever excluded from political power in the community expressed a concern shared by most Anglican churchmen in Ireland. Swift's convictions added up to the following : he accepted the Revolution, he disavowed with true Whiggish fervour the doctrine of passive obedience and non-resistance, he was naturally at home in that body of political theory standing in opposition to the doctrine of absolutism ; at the same time he was one of unyielding loyalty to the Established Church, willing to accept toleration for the Protestant Nonconformists, but bitterly opposed to any change in the existing laws which were designed to exclude them from political office. In holding to this particular combination of beliefs Swift was not unique, but his point of view was one more commonly met with in Dublin than in London. His problem, which the course taken by events in England during the opening decade of the century pointed up with increasing emphasis, was to define a political-religious relationship which would preserve all of his principles and still accord with the temper and realities of the time.

The first opportunity to comment on the problems of the day presented itself shortly after Swift's return to England in the company of the Earl of Berkeley in April 1701. On this occasion the questions at issue were entirely political in nature. For some months now Tory power had been on the rise, Somers and other Lords of the Whig Junto had been dismissed from the Ministry, and the elections of February 1701 had resulted in a marked increase of Tory strength in the House of Commons. It was at this juncture that the Tories in the lower House undertook to impeach Somers, along with Orford, Halifax, and the Earl of Portland, for acts done while in office. Swift not only shared the resentment felt by all the Whigs, but was fearful lest this display of extreme partisanship disrupt the nation at a moment of growing peril from abroad. His *Contests and Dissensions* was a timely and effective statement delivered from the Whig point of view—a warning to the Tories not to carry party zeal to dangerous lengths, a warning to the country as a whole to preserve those checks and balances which ensured the unity of the national community. But it was something more than an occasional pamphlet. It contained a historical and theoretical analysis of political behaviour, and its wide sweep showed what good use Swift had made of his opportunity while at Moor Park to talk, and read, and think systematically about all the topics which the European mind of that time regarded as falling within the field of political speculation. Swift also found occasion to introduce into his analysis his characteristic view of Puritanism as a form of tyranny. Indeed, had the Whigs who roundly applauded his pamphlet considered it more carefully they might have found things in it to give them pause, but it was so timely a defence of Somers and the other Whig Lords and so firmly grounded in Whig political principles that his uncharitable words about the entire

F

Puritan tradition went seemingly unobserved. The *Contests and Dissensions* was not the place to enter upon a discussion of Church and State in relation to one another, but in setting forth his political credo Swift did not conceal, on the contrary he voiced quite emphatically, the hostility which as an Anglican churchman he bore towards all Nonconformists.

Of his next visit to England, which occurred in 1702, little is known. Apparently the Whigs now conveyed their thanks to the author of the *Contests and Dissensions*, but they seem to have done little else. Either because no occasion existed or because Swift did not choose to find one he remained silent on public affairs. But during his stay in England from November 1703 through May 1704 his concern over the political-religious questions then under dispute is reflected in his correspondence. The Tories had introduced a bill to prohibit Occasional Conformity, the device whereby a Dissenter, if he could bring himself to attend an Anglican service and take the sacrament there, could circumvent the Test Act and qualify for political office. The bill was of course designed to bear hard upon the Nonconformists, and the Whigs had promptly rallied to oppose this Tory move. Here was a rare opportunity for some writer to make his fortune with the Whigs—some writer possessing precisely the sort of talent which the author of the *Contests and Dissensions* had displayed two years previously. Swift, however, was not happy over the turn that matters were taking. After all, would not the Tories' bill advance the interests of the Church? He was told by both Somers and Bishop Burnet that it would not, but he remained unconvinced by their assurances. 'I know not what to think, and therefore shall think no more', he wrote to a friend in Ireland. At the last minute—just before the defeat of the bill—he was apparently prevailed on to come out in support of the Whig position, but his pamphlet never appeared. 'It came too late by a day,' he explained to his correspondent, 'so I could not print it.' He was still a Whig, but a Whig upon his own somewhat unusual terms, as he was now beginning to realize more and more.

It was during his long residence in England from the autumn of 1707 to the summer of 1709 that he seems to have arrived at a full understanding of what his position carried with it in the way of theory, and of the line of action it suggested. He now set to work upon a series of pamphlets which he proposed to bring out together in a single volume. The most important of these new writings was the *Sentiments of a Church-of-England Man*, a statement of basic political and church principles carrying with it a definite theory of relationship between Church and State. Swift had chosen his ground carefully. He was now first and foremost the Churchman, and as such he was resolved to keep clear of all purely partisan doctrines. He would protect the Established Church against all efforts to weaken its position. It was not necessary to affirm that it was a divinely established institution (though Swift never asserted that it was not); it was sufficient to show that it stood by virtue of the rational will of the nation as a whole. The Church, that is, was independent in the sense that it lay outside the area within which party strife occurred. We know that at least three other pamphlets of his were taking shape at about this same time. The *Remarks Upon a Book, Intitled, 'The Rights of the Christian Church Asserted'* was an answer to Matthew Tindall, whose controversial volume had appeared in 1706. Here Swift's purpose was to disprove Tindall's contention that religion is a mere contrivance of the civil power, and he went further than in the *Sentiments* in suggesting that the Church is a divine institution, but as in that pamphlet his principal concern was, again, to establish what might be called the rational independence of the Church: the civil power may clearly interfere with the Church in any number of ways, but it is apparent in reason that it can never of itself perform the Church's offices. The *Project for the Advancement of Religion and the Reformation of Manners* was a reforming tract in which he succeeded in being witty without sacrificing anything in the way of sincerity. *An Argument against Abolishing Christianity* was in a still different vein—ironic disputation serving the double purpose of heaping ridicule upon the deists and advancing in a novel way —a fashionably paradoxical way—the practical advantages of maintaining the Church.

Of these pamphlets only the *Project* was published during this 1707-1709 period. The *Sentiments* and the *Argument* appeared in 1711 (in his *Miscellanies in Prose and Verse*), by which time he had gone over to the Tories. The *Remarks* did not see the light until 1763. What, it would be interesting to know, had happened to his original plan for publication? His correspondence gives no clear answer. But in the meantime a situation had arisen which had called forth immediate action from him. At the end of October 1708 the Whig Ministry had been further strengthened by a number of changes, one of which placed the Earl of Wharton in office as Lord Lieutenant of Ireland—a clear sign that the repeal of the Test Act in Ireland had been determined upon as a preliminary step towards relieving the Dissenters in England. From Swift's point of view this was the worst thing that could happen, and accordingly he immediately drew up another pamphlet, *A Letter from a Member of the House of Commons in Ireland to a Member of the House of Commons in England, Concerning the Sacramental Test*, which he published before the year's end. Purporting, as its title shows, to be from the pen of a member of the Irish House of Commons, it was the clearest warning to the Whig Ministry that their intended course of action in Ireland would be fiercely resisted there, and a blunt reminder that the friends of the Church of Ireland were Whigs almost to a man. Swift's last pamphlet before his shift in political allegiance was apparently written early in 1710 after his return to Ireland but does not seem to have been published at the time. It is entitled *A Letter to a Member of Parliament in Ireland. Upon the chusing a new Speaker there*, and urges that every effort be made to secure as speaker one who will resist all efforts to remove the Test Act.

Such, in brief, are the circumstances surrounding Swift's earliest public writings. Even though our interest in his pamphlets may not be that of the historian of this period, for whom they are documents of genuine importance, we are still under the necessity, if we are going to have any opinion about them at all, of establishing in some detail the background of events against which they lie. To understand Swift's ideas on politics and the Church is to understand how they took shape in his mind under the pressure of contemporary events. But there are other aspects of these pamphlets—aspects of greater interest to the general reader. Swift's theories on Church and State are so important a part of the man that they can almost be said to be a key to his personality. Besides this, they have that imaginative scope that we find in a writer like Hobbes—that sense of the world's body and the entire human situation. These pamphlets are also examples of effective public writing, and though the mighty controversialist of the Oxford Ministry has not yet appeared upon the scene we have a master of clear, forcible exposition. And if we look closely enough, we shall also discover the hand of that satiric artist who had already produced a masterpiece in the *Tale of a Tub*. Here, to be sure, he was working in quite a different medium, but in both the *Project for the Advancement of Religion* and the *Argument against Abolishing Christianity* various modes of irony are introduced, while impersonation is employed in the *Letter concerning the Sacramental Test* if not also in the *Sentiments of a Church-of-England Man*.

The *Contests and Dissensions* is perfectly straightforward in both style and manner of address. Nothing of importance attaches to the author himself; he sometimes speaks in the first person, but his tone and point of view are entirely impersonal. It is an even-tempered appraisal of the dangers raised by the impeachment of the Whig Lords, and is backed by a broad and inclusive theory of government and the state. By drawing upon Greek and Roman political history, Swift—or should we say the writer?—brings forward many telling analogies between the ancient world and modern England and suggests a number of historical parallels between famous Athenian figures and the Whig Lords now suffering under the Tories' retributive action. Swift was ready for his subject. He knew Temple's work, he was thoroughly familiar with both classical and Whig political theories, he was at about this same time making a study of the growth of the English Constitution and parliamentary government, and under the stimulus of Hobbes and others he had formed his own psychological theory of individual and group behaviour.

The pamphlet was written and published for one clear purpose, that being to strike a timely blow in behalf of the Whig cause, and was Whig in thought and sentiment. Swift was not here concerned with how the state comes into being but with the power that *is* the state. This power, as he knew if only from Temple, is absolute, unlimited, and resides in the entire community—in the 'Body of a People'. But its location is not the same as the forms under which it expends itself in action : it can fall into the hands of one person, of a few men, or of the many ; but it is the mixed monarchial state which proves best in practice—a state in which the power is held in balance between King, Nobles, and Commons (between, that is, the one, the few, the many). When this balance is broken,

whether by the Negligence, Folly, or Weakness of the Hand that held it, or by mighty Weights fallen into either Scale; the Power will never continue long in equal Division between the two remaining Parties, but (until the Ballance is fixed anew) will run entirely into one. This gives the truest Account of what is understood in the most ancient and approved *Greek* Authors, by the Word *Tyranny* . . .[1]

It follows that tyranny is not necessarily the usurping rule of a single person. There can just as well be an oligarchical tyranny or a tyranny of the many, though both of these latter forms yield in time to the single tyrant. Since the stability and longevity of the state depend upon a maintenance of the balance between the three practical elements, any altercation between these elements endangers the whole mechanism. Thus Swift admonished the Tory House of Commons, which he represented as engaged in a struggle for power with the Lords—a struggle of the Many against the Few. It is amusing to remember that in his first public utterance on politics he was representing the Tories as dangerous democrats.

At least three different strains of thought came together in this discourse of his.[2] One, going back to Polybius, was the classical theory of the monarchial mixed state, a theory which had been set forth by English writers before, during, and after the period which saw the Puritans in power. Another strain is to be found in Whig speculation of the post-Restoration decades, which retained the theory of a balance of power between the three elements in the state but looked for early examples of this kind of mixed monarchy to what were pictured as the 'Gothic' states of northern Europe. This theory went on to represent English constitutional government as Gothic in origin, with the conclusion that it had from the first taken the form of a mixed—and therefore limited—monarchy. Throughout the *Contests and*

[1] *The Contests and Dissensions in Athens and Rome*, chap. I.

[2] On Swift's political theory, Professor Z. S. Fink is enlightening; see his 'Political Theory in *Gulliver's Travels*', *English Literary History*, XIV (1947), 151-61. See also Irvin Ehrenpreis, 'Swift on Liberty', *Journal of the History of Ideas*, XIII (1952), 131-46; and Samuel Kliger, *The Goths in England, A Study in Seventeenth and Eighteenth Century Thought* (Cambridge, Mass., 1952).

Dissensions Swift is leaning heavily upon the classical tradition, and at one point—in Chapter I—he seems to dismiss the 'Gothic' theory, but he was thoroughly grounded in both and on a much later occasion told Pope that he 'adored the wisdom' of 'that Gothic Institution' which made Parliaments annual. But Swift also knew Hobbes. True, he regarded him as one of evil counsel and rejected utterly the Hobbesian theory of absolute government—after all, the *Contests and Dissensions* was a warning against embarking upon a course which could easily lead to some form of absolutism. However, Swift was not one to pass over Hobbes's realistic analysis of motive and behaviour in favour of any of the more genial views of human conduct then current. There is in all men and in all groups of men a fundamental desire for power ; this is endless and exorbitant, and it must be circumvented. Whereas for Hobbes the circumvention lay in the delegation of all power to a single authority, for Swift it meant a balancing of powers between the three orders in the state. By maintaining such a balance, and only in this way, could society hope to avoid tyranny, the greatest of all evils. It is to be observed how, in Swift's political thought, this element of pessimism similar to what is found in Hobbes came to be joined with something like confidence in man's ability, through the application of reason and common sense, to control his own disruptive passion for endless power. The balance between the one, the few, and the many was in reality a check upon the innate selfishness of the individual and the special group :

this must be said in Behalf of human Kind; that common Sense, and plain Reason, while Men are disengaged from acquired Opinions, will ever have some general Influence upon their Minds . . .[1]

The whole art of politics lay in bringing experience and common sense to bear upon the problem of preserving this equilibrium, this check, for as long a period of time as

[1] *The Contests and Dissensions in Athens and Rome*, chap. V.

possible. Everything that Swift ever uttered on the subject of government and political theory was for the purpose of winning more time for the ordered state, of fighting off the moment—probably inevitable—of its declination into one of the several forms of tyranny. Swift's view of the historical pattern of Western civilization and of the future which men could look forward to was again derived from the political writers of the classical tradition, who assumed a periodic rise and fall of nations and governments to be a natural law, but encouraged men with the thought that through the exercise of art and prudence it might be possible to prolong the life of a particular state almost indefinitely. Swift's statement on this matter, found towards the beginning of Chapter V, is of crucial importance:

The Fate of Empire is grown a common Place: That all Forms of Government having been instituted by Men, must be mortal like their Authors, and have their Periods of Duration limited, as well as those of private Persons; this is a Truth of vulgar Knowledge and Observation. But there are few who turn their Thoughts to examine how these Diseases in a State are bred, that hasten its End. . . . For, although we cannot prolong the Period of a Commonwealth beyond the Decree of Heaven, or the Date of its Nature, any more than human Life, beyond the Strength of the Seminal Virtue; yet we may manage a sickly Constitution, and preserve a strong one; we may watch and prevent Accidents; we may turn off a great Blow from without, and purge away an ill Humour that is lacking within: And by these and other such Methods, render a State long-lived, although not immortal. Yet some Physicians have thought, that if it were practicable to keep the several Humours of the Body in an exact equal Ballance of each with its Opposite, it might be immortal; and so perhaps would a political Body, if the Ballance of Power could be always held exactly even. But I doubt, this is as almost impossible in the Practice as the other.

At one point only did Swift, in the *Contests and Dissensions*, express sentiments to which any of those who numbered themselves among the Whigs could have taken exception.

In his concluding chapter he inserted a brief review of constitutional history since the Conquest. On the subject of James II and the Revolution he was orthodox enough: through the weakness of Charles II and his brother James the balance had been put in danger, but this peril had been 'very seasonably prevented by the late Revolution'. It was his treatment of the Puritan régime of the mid-seventeenth century that marked him out as one whose commitment to the Whig theory of the state did not entail any modification of High-Church animosities. The middle of the Elizabethan era, he wrote, saw the power of Nobles and Commons perfectly balanced, but the Puritan faction arose thereafter and at length overthrew the Constitution and 'according to the usual Course of such Revolution, did introduce a Tyranny, first of the People, and then of a single Person'.

The *Contests and Dissensions* has a youthful quality all its own. Swift had an instinctive feeling for the rhetoric of controversy, and in this earliest pamphlet of his he was already shaping his material and his phrases for the immediate purpose in hand and the audience to be dealt with. But in spite of such self-imposed restraint something of a young man's enthusiasm for ideas in general and his own particular doctrines runs through the discourse. Others might have their systems of beliefs and their projects; this was his—the concept of rational freedom, its history, and the way to maintain it. √The *Sentiments of a Church-of-England Man, With Respect to Religion and Government* is clearly the work of an older writer. Broader in scope, completely efficient in its easy, almost conversational style, it is the most impressive statement of his position on Church and State ever to come from his pen. It is, indeed, much more than a statement of personal beliefs. We have seen that it develops a concept of Anglicanism designed to enable the Church to preserve its own independence while at the same time accepting the Revolution both in fact and in respect of underlying political theory. Writing in 1708, Swift had every reason to be aware of the controversial aspects of his subject, and his pamphlet was undoubtedly intended as a warning to the Ministry against tampering with the Test Act in Ireland. But he chose to lay his views before the reader in a calm, conciliatory manner that seemed to place his whole discussion quite outside the realm of heated controversy. His thesis here was that the views held by the extremists of both parties should be discounted. This was now—in 1708—Swift's own belief. Not only did the classical tradition in political theory teach that partisanship was likely to endanger the balance within the state, but his own experiences in England since the time of *Contests and Dissensions* had been leading him towards a position based upon loyalty to the Church rather than to either party. He was entirely sincere, therefore, in adopting throughout the *Sentiments* a neutral attitude towards Whigs and Tories. The pamphlet bears no name. The writer represents himself as a 'private Man'—a Church-of-England man, of course—seeking to render his country true service 'by unbiassing his Mind as much as possible, and thus endeavouring to moderate between the Rival Powers'. He goes out of the way to call our attention to his anonymity: he has chosen to conceal his name, he tells us, so that no one may think that in expressing these sentiments of his he is in search of any political favours. It was Swift's practice to give such a supposed writer a fully established character. In this instance, however, one speaks of impersonation in the sense of self-impersonation, for Swift and his Church-of-England man who is unbiasing his mind as much as possible of purely party opinions were almost identical.

The first part of the pamphlet is a summary of the writer's religious views. Concerning Episcopacy, he is 'sure it is most agreeable to primitive Institution', though he will not attempt to determine whether it be of Divine Right. He would prefer that rites, ceremonies, and forms of prayer be determined by the clergy, but he will accept the direction

of the legislature in regard to things in their own nature
indifferent if Christians may thereby be united. As to sects
and toleration : because sects have arisen they must now be
accepted, and he is willing to accord them toleration ; but
since these sects still design the destruction of the Church
they must, though tolerated, be excluded from power. To
Swift this was no manner of persecution ; it was the only
way to maintain that balance by which freedom was assured
to the nation as a whole. So completely were Reason and
Nature—the normal, the healthy, the right—identified in
his mind with uniformity ! Sects, we are told,

seem only tolerated, with any Reason, because they are already
spread ; and because it would not be agreeable with so mild a Government, or so pure a Religion as ours, to use violent Methods against
great Numbers of *mistaken* People, while they do not manifestly
endanger the Constitution of either. But the greatest Advocates for
general Liberty of Conscience, will allow that they ought to be
checked in their Beginnings, if they will allow them to be an Evil
of all ; or, which is the same Thing, if they will only grant, it were
better for the Peace of the State, that there should be none.[1]

And again :

[The Church-of-England man] is very far from closing with the
new Opinion of those, who would make [Schism] no Crime at all ;
and argue at a wild Rate, that God Almighty is delighted with the
Variety of Faith and Worship, as he is with the Varieties of Nature.[2]

Swift's steadfast unwillingness to accept more than a limited
form of toleration for the Dissenters arose in part, it is
apparent, from his conviction that diversity of beliefs constituted a practical danger to the ordered, balanced state.
But even stronger and more deeply rooted was his fear of
diversity in and for itself : marked differences of belief
could only, it seemed to him, spring from irrational sources,
since men in their natural disposition—normal men—inevitably found themselves in substantial agreement. As we

[1] *The Sentiments of a Church-of-England Man*, Sect. I.   [2] ibid., sect. I.

follow Swift's discussion of this all-important matter we are naturally reminded, by contrast, of the views ultimately arrived at by John Milton. For the great Puritan, Truth was conceived of, to be sure, as an absolute thing, but it was an absolute which unfolded itself to human creatures through a variety of religious beliefs—a progressive revelation by God to a humanity struggling on its journey through the Valley of Time and Experience. Swift is unquestionably diminished in modern eyes by reason of his steadfast adherence to the principle of uniformity. Yet it is unfair to overlook the fact that he, no less than John Milton, was moved by a concept of human freedom. And I think this should be added: however repellent Swift's policy of restriction may seem to us today, we have to acknowledge that there was never anything of the bully or the sadist about him. He defined his grounds. He gave fair warning where and when he would strike. And he *was* striking in behalf of a theory of liberty which has its recognized place in our western tradition. The closing words of his great epitaph —the admonition to imitate, if we can, one who fought with his entire strength for the cause of freedom—are more than magnificent rhetoric.

The second section of the *Sentiments* sets forth the writer's convictions with respect to government. The main points are much the same as those which had already been made in *Contests and Dissensions*. 'Arbitrary Power' is the great evil to be avoided. We have arbitrary power when 'any one *Person*, or *Body* of Men, who do not represent the *Whole*, seize into their Hands the Power in the last Resort'. Swift never showed much interest in the various theories of the time concerning the mechanism or sequence of events giving rise to the ordered state. Here in the *Sentiments* he touched more directly on these topics than was his custom. The savage life is marked by anarchy. The first step away from his condition is through some early form of arbitrary power. Thereafter comes the ordered state, which is one wherein freedom has been established through the adjustment, the balancing of power, all this being 'an Effect and Consequence of mature Thinking'. Swift was neither a primitivist, finding in man's earliest condition the happiest period of human existence, nor a progressivist, confident that the Earthly Paradise would come to pass as the future unfolded itself. The good life—such as it could be for a limited creature like man—was here and now. But as between the life of the savages and any later phase of society in which men have lost the freedom that was once theirs and find themselves condemned to live in slavery, the advantage lay with the primitive, anarchic condition of life.

The Church-of-England man is confident that the fundamentals of government to which he subscribes are shared by all reasonable Whigs and Tories. He does not believe that among established governments there is one species more pleasing to God than another—a declaration which was of course an explicit denial of the pre-Revolution Tory theory of the English monarchy. And he proceeds to reject, vigorously and at some length, the doctrine of passive obedience. On the subject of non-resistance he offers an interpretation which brings this latter doctrine into accord with the theory of the mixed state: the supreme magistrate to whom obedience is always due is not a single person nor a representative of the purely executive power in the state, but the absolute and unlimited legislative power residing in the whole people. He ends on the dominant note of moderation, expressing the conviction that whoever desires to 'preserve the Constitution entire in Church and State' will be sure to avoid the extremes of Whig for the sake of the Church, the extremes of Tory on account of the State.

Of the five other prose works of this period, the *Project for the Advancement of Religion* and the *Argument against Abolishing Christianity* retain for present-day readers an interest beyond what attaches to them in the way of historical significance. In both we find the kind of public

writing Swift excelled at—writing that is effective because
of arresting manner or provocative wit. There can be little
doubt that the *Project* was perfectly understood in its own
day. It was a reforming tract—the type was well-known—
and the author's sincerity was never in question. Swift's
old patron, the Earl of Berkeley, expressed the hope that
with the co-operation of the bookseller and the Archbishop
of York the Queen might come into possession of a copy,
for he was entirely of the opinion, so he wrote, 'that her
Majesty's reading of the book of the Project for the increase
of Morality and Piety, may be of very great use to that end'.
And in the newly-launched *Tatler* Steele had words of praise
for it. Nevertheless, it has deceived at least one modern
commentator, who has taken it as another example of
Swiftian irony, and while the professed purpose of the tract
and the moral judgements which it contains are—contrary
to any such view—entirely unambiguous, it is not without
a sub-ironic quality. A serious project put forward by the
author of the *Tale of a Tub* cannot very well help raising
a question in our minds until we see that the *Project* before
us is from the pen of another of Swift's fictional characters.
This time we have a 'person of quality'. He agrees with
us that it is indeed an age of projects, but he has observed
that 'there have never been any for the Improvement of
Religion and Morals'. We are, as it were, forewarned
against the enthusiasm which is inevitably in store for us
if the *Project* runs true to form. Another strain of what is
close to irony results from the fact that our person of quality
is no clergyman, ignorant of the vices of the age and easily
shocked, but one who knows as much about the sins and
follies of the fashionable world as the next gentleman and is
able to discourse on them in language that any wit might use :

[today men] never go about, as in former Times, to hide or palliate
their Vices; but expose them freely to View, like any other common
Occurrences of Life, without the least Reproach from the World,
or themselves. For Instance, any Man will tell you, he intends to

be drunk this Evening, or was so last Night, with as little Ceremony or Scruple, as he would tell you the Time of the Day. He will let you know he is going to a Wench, or that he has got a Clap; with as much Indifferency as he would a Piece of publick News. He will swear, curse, or blaspheme, without the least Passion or Provocation. And, although all Regard for Reputation be not quite laid aside in the other Sex; it is, however, at so low an Ebb, that very few among them, seem to think Virtue and Conduct of any Necessity for preserving it.

The point upon which this entire plan for advancing religion and reforming manners is made to turn is self-interest: if the administrative branch of government—the Queen, that is—can be persuaded to advance those of exemplary conduct, then there is a fair chance that religion may become 'the Turn and Fashion of the Age'. The writer is aware that his suggestion may be looked upon as one likely to promote hypocrisy, and hypocrisy may be one of the results, he grants; but 'if One in Twenty should be brought over to true Piety by this, or the like Methods, and the other Nineteen be only Hypocrites, the Advantage would still be great'. Reasoning like this—need we remind ourselves?—is reasoning which has been carefully adjusted to the world of fashion. It is almost as though some character in a comedy of manners were holding forth. If the outside never corresponds to the inside, hypocrisy as such need not concern us. Or again, if outward dress is all there is, if clothes are the mind and the soul, what is virtue but appearance? Swift and Shaw inhabited totally different moral worlds, but the Swiftian comedy of ideas is like the Shavian in that its wit and paradoxes have their source in dramatic situation.

In the *Argument against Abolishing Christianity* the ironic disputation is carried on with an *élan* that reminds us of parts of the *Tale of a Tub*. There is a release of energy made possible by the fact that we have left sober reality and every-day logic behind us. We are in a world which becomes more curious with every extension of the argument. For this effect Swift, in the present instance, is relying less upon the character of the writer—though this writer speaks in the first person throughout the opening paragraphs and establishes his identity—than upon paradoxical argument as such. We are reminded that this is a 'wise and paradoxical Age'. The *Argument* is thus adjusted by design to the modern spirit, though the writer is fully conscious that his attempt to show that there is yet no 'absolute Necessity of extirpating the Christian Religion' may prove to be too great a paradox even for such times. So the argument begins. But the question soon arises as to what is here being defended. Not real Christianity, we are assured.

I hope, no Reader imagines me so weak to stand up in the Defence of *real* Christianity; such as used in primitive Times (if we may believe the Authors of those Ages) to have an Influence upon Mens Belief and Actions: To offer at the Restoring of that, would indeed be a wild Project; it would be to dig up Foundations; to destroy at one Blow *all* the Wit, and *half* the Learning of the Kingdom; to break the entire Frame and Constitution of Things; to ruin Trade, extinguish Arts and Sciences with the Professors of them; in short, to turn our Courts, Exchanges and Shops into Desarts . . .

It is exuberance like this that carries the argument along from one paradox to the next, then through the refutation of some eight arguments advanced by those who favour abolition, and finally through a closing summary of the various inconveniences likely to follow upon the disappearance of Christianity.

The three remaining pieces—*Remarks upon Tindall's 'The Rights of the Christian Church Asserted'*, the *Letter Concerning the Sacramental Test*, and the *Letter to a Member of Parliament*—do not call for much in the way of commentary. The *Remarks*, aimed not only at Tindall but also at the other deistic writers of the time who had come to be associated with him, contains the wonderfully turned passage in which Swift is paying his respects to all these latter-day opponents :

And truly when I compare the former Enemies to Christianity, such as *Socinus*, *Hobbes*, and *Spinosa*; with such of their Successors, as *Toland*, *Asgil*, *Coward*, *Gildon*, this Author of the *Rights*, and some others; the Church appeareth to me like the sick old Lion in the Fable, who, after having his Person outraged by the Bull, the Elephant, and Horse, and the Bear, took nothing so much to Heart, as to find himself at last insulted by the Spurn of an Ass.

As has already been pointed out, Swift affirms in the course of the *Remarks* his belief in the divine origins of the Church. He is the Whig in acknowledging the supreme legislative power of the Body of the People ; yet the Church, dependent for its legal status on the good will of the community, possesses a rational independence which no power on earth can change :

Put the Case, that walking on the slack Rope were the only Talent required by Act of Parliament for making a Man a Bishop; no Doubt, when a Man had done his Feat of Activity in Form, he might sit in the House of Lords, put on his Robes and his Rotchet, go down to his Palace, receive and spend his Rents; but it requireth very little Christianity to believe this Tumbler to be one whit more a Bishop than he was before; because the Law of God hath otherwise decreed; which Law, although a Nation may refuse to receive it, cannot alter in its own Nature.

The *Letter Concerning the Sacramental Test* was necessarily anonymous, since it was supposedly written by 'a Member of the House of Commons in Ireland to a Member of the House of Commons in England'. In the earlier editions (the first appeared in December 1708), Swift exploited this anonymous situation in order to make ironic commentary upon his own loyalty to the Church in comparison with the willingness of Dr. Ralph Lambert, Wharton's recently-chosen chaplain, to comply with the Ministry's prevailing views. The writer of the *Letter* makes reference to '*Two*

Divines of this Kingdom now in *London*', and expresses his confidence that Lambert, always strong for the Test, will never change his position, though it remains to be seen how the 'other Divine' will conduct himself! But such irony was incidental. Swift was in deadly earnest, and to meet the danger which Wharton as Lord Lieutenant seemed to pose he fell back upon the direct, forcible style which was always at his command. It was only necessary to have the writer of the *Letter* set forth in all bluntness the doctrines which Swift had been expounding in his other pamphlets : the Whigs in Ireland are for the Church of England no less than for King William and the Revolution ; the Dissenters have toleration ; what else do they want?

. . . there is one small Doubt I would be willingly satisfied in, before I agree to the repealing of the *Test*; that is, whether these same Protestants, when they have, by their Dexterity, made themselves the National Religion, and disposed the Church Revenues among their *Pastors* or *Themselves*, will be so kind to allow *us Dissenters*, I do not say a Share in Employments, but a bare *Toleration* by Law.

The *Letter to a Member of Parliament in Ireland. Upon Chusing a new Speaker there*, written in 1710 while Swift was in Ireland, is short and to the purpose. The writer desires to put his correspondent on guard against the 'High-flying Whigs', and goes on to admonish his friends in Ireland to choose as a speaker one who can be counted on to resist the efforts about to be made to secure a repeal of the Test.

Save that they were written by one known as a Whig, one increasingly associated in the public mind with other Whig writers like Addison and Steele, the purely literary compositions and *jeux d'esprit* of this 1699-1710 period are, with a few minor exceptions, free of all political implications. The amusing *Meditation on a Broomstick*, the earlier portion of the *Thoughts on Various Subjects*, and the *Tritical Essay upon the Faculties of the Mind* were apparently composed at various times between 1702 and 1707, and all were printed in 1711 in Swift's *Miscellanies* (the *Meditation* had previously appeared in 1710 in an unauthorized edition by Curll). It has now been established that the *Story of the Injured Lady*, which was not published until 1746, must have been written in 1707. Its interest for us lies in its showing at how early a period Swift's resentment at England's treatment of Ireland had become articulate. The Bickerstaff papers were appearing in 1708 and 1709. There are, finally, the poems of this period, the best of which, most would agree, are *Mrs. Harris's Petition*, the earlier, unrevised version of *Baucis and Philemon*, and *A Description of the Morning*. Much of his verse appeared for the first time in the 1711 *Miscellanies*, though five poems (including the *Petition*, the *Description*, and a revised version of *Baucis and Philemon*) found their way into print in 1709 or 1710.

It need scarcely be pointed out that it was the Partridge affair that gave rise to Swift's most famous impersonation. John Partridge was a well-known astrologer who had been issuing his annual almanac, *Merlinus Liberatus*, since 1680, and had long since become fair game for the London wits. Swift, who contemned him both for the manner in which he played upon vulgar superstition and for his anti-clerical utterances, proceeded to deal with him on the latter's own ground. The first step was to create in Isaac Bickerstaff a rival astrologer. This done, the rest followed according to the logic of the devised situation. Bickerstaff's *Predictions for the Year 1708* appeared before the end of January 1708, and among other things foretold the death of John Partridge on the ensuing twenty-ninth of March, 'about eleven at Night'. Two publications, both appearing at the very end of March, announced triumphantly that Partridge had died almost on schedule. One of these, *An Elegy on Mr. Patrige*, was in doggerel verse. The other, *The Accomplishment of the First of Mr. Bickerstaff's Predictions*, was cast in the form of a 'Letter to a Person of Honour' and contained an account of the circumstances surrounding Partridge's death as observed by the writer—still another character—and reported to the noble lord in whose employment he had been acting. Bickerstaff made a second appearance early in 1709 in the *Vindication of Isaac Bickerstaff, Esq.*, where, by means of the kind of logic which was controlling the entire farce, he had little difficulty in turning Partridge's own protestations that he was still alive into proof that he must be dead. *A Famous Prediction of Merlin, the British Wizard*—a mixture of verse and prose—brought Swift's part to a close.

The earliest example of Swift's mature manner in poetry is generally thought to be *Verses Wrote in a Lady's Ivory Table-Book* (1698?), to which reference has been made in the preceding chapter. *Mrs. Harris's Petition* was written early in 1701 shortly before the expiration of Berkeley's appointment as a Lord Justice, and gives an incomparable picture of social life in Dublin Castle. The interminable Mistress Frances Harris, gentlewoman to Lady Berkeley, is holding forth on a recent misadventure of hers. Before she manages to come to a stop, we have been introduced to half the staff of servants—Mary the housemaid; Mrs. Dukes, wife of one of the footmen; Whittle, the valet; Dame Wadgar, the deaf housekeeper; Cary, clerk of the kitchen; and Ferris, the steward. Life below stairs in an Irish household has provided a rich theme for more than one modern novelist. Was Swift anticipated in his use of such a subject? This poem is also memorable for the description it gives of the chaplain at the Castle, now also the vicar of Laracor:

> So the *Chaplain* came in; now the Servants
> say, he is my Sweet-heart,
> Because he's always in my Chamber, and I
> always take his Part;
> So, as the *Devil* would have it, before I was aware,
> out I blunder'd,
> *Parson*, said I, can you cast a *Nativity*, when a
> Body's plunder'd?

(Now you must know, he hates to be call'd *Parson*,
    like the *Devil*.)
Truly, says he, Mrs. *Nab*, it might become you
    to be more civil:
If your Money be gone, as a Learned *Divine* says,
    d'ye see,
You are no *Text* for my Handling, so take that
    from me:
I was never taken for a *Conjurer* before, I'd
    have you to know.
Lord, said I, don't be angry, I'm sure I never
    thought you so;
You know, I honour the Cloth, I design to be
    a *Parson's* Wife,
I never took one in *Your Coat* for a *Conjurer* in
    all my Life.
With that, he twisted his Girdle at me like a
    Rope, as who should say,
Now you may go hang your self for me, and
    so went away.

Baucis and Philemon, Swift's fine imitation of Ovid, we have in two versions. The earlier of these, dating from 1706 and preserved in manuscript, is much the better one. The published version had undergone extensive revision under the eyes of Addison, but—according to our modern taste—suffered markedly in the process.

It was early in April 1709 that Steele launched his *Tatler*, and by adopting Isaac Bickerstaff as his pseudonym gave renewed life to Swift's already famous character. Swift undoubtedly assisted his friend Steele in more ways than one in this new venture, but his first full-scale contribution seems to have been the *Description of the Morning*, which appeared in the *Tatler* No. 9 (30 April). It is one of Swift's minor triumphs. Any work of art which discloses a point of view markedly individualistic or eccentric partakes of a certain dramatic quality: it is not the artist's presence that we are aware of so much as that of some person who is forcing us to experience the world on his terms. When the verses appeared in the *Tatler* Isaac Bickerstaff took occasion to explain that they were the work of a kinsman of his who liked to describe in his poetry exactly what he was used to finding in real life; he never, so the readers were told, 'forms fields, or nymphs, or groves, where they are not', and it was to be observed that the present verses were not only a description of the morning, but of the morning in town, 'nay, of the morning at this end of the town, where my kinsman at present lodges'. The wit and humour of this well-known *genre*-piece derive not only from the fact that it is anti-poetry from beginning to end but from the assurance with which Bickerstaff's kinsman has established his point of view and proceeded to bring all the details into accord with his curious perspective.

> Now hardly here and there an Hackney-Coach
> Appearing, show'd the Ruddy Morns Approach.
> Now *Betty* from her Masters Bed had flown,
> And softly stole to discompose her own.
> The Slipshod Prentice from his Masters Door
> Had par'd the Dirt, and Sprinkled round the Floor.
> Now *Moll* had whirl'd her Mop with dext'rous Airs,
> Prepar'd to Scrub the Entry and the Stairs.
> The Youth with Broomy Stumps began to trace
> The Kennel-Edge, where Wheels had worn the Place.
> The Smallcoat-Man was heard with Cadence deep,
> 'Till drown'd in Shriller Notes of Chimney-Sweep.
> Duns at his Lordships Gate began to meet,
> And Brickdust *Moll* had Scream'd through half the Street.

V

TORY JOURNALIST

It was on 31 August 1710 that Swift left Ireland aboard the Lord Lieutenant's yacht, having been empowered by the Irish clergy to take up with the new Ministry the matter of the First Fruits. He landed at Parkgate the following day, and was in London by 7 September. There was an air of excitement and suspense everywhere, for as yet no one could tell how far the political reaction against the late Godolphin Ministry was likely to go, and Swift suddenly found himself an object of solicitation by both parties. The Whigs—so he wrote to his superior, Archbishop King of Dublin—looked upon him 'as a sort of bough for drowning men to lay hold of'; the Tories regarded him 'as one discontented with the late men in power' and therefore 'ready to approve present things'. Swift hesitated for some days. Directly after his arrival in London he had had a most unsatisfactory conference with the fallen Godolphin, whose coldness so enraged him that, as he told Stella, he was 'almost vowing revenge'. But such thoughts were temporarily put aside when he was with Addison and Steele, and he was willing enough to assist the latter with the *Tatler*, to which he now contributed a paper on stylistic matters (No. 230, 28 Sept.) and a second poem, the capital *Description of a City Shower* (No. 238, 17 Oct.). At the end of his first fortnight in London he was trying to convince himself that the present political struggle left one in his position—a position he had defined so often in the preceding years—quite untouched. 'We shall have a strange Winter here,' he wrote in the *Journal* on 20 September, 'between the struggles of a cunning provoked discarded party, and the triumphs of one in power; of both which

I shall be an indifferent spectator . . .' If the blandishments
of the Tories, and of Harley particularly, finally won Swift
over to the new Ministry, it was the rebuff administered
by Godolphin which first caused him to give up his attitude of neutrality. As he brooded over the reception he
had had from Godolphin—'altogether short, dry, and
morose'—his long impatience with the Whig policy in
matters of religion and his mounting indignation against
those chiefly responsible for this policy now came to a point
of concentrated fury, and in the closing days of September
he was at work on a scurrilous lampoon aimed at the fallen
minister. *The Virtues of Sid Hamet the Magician's Rod*,
appearing in the first part of October, was Swift's declaration of war against the Whigs.

It did not take Harley long to induce Swift to go still
further. The two had their first meeting on 4 October,
they met again for a long conference three days later, and
before the end of the month Swift had taken over the editorship of the weekly *Examiner*. In the course of these early
conversations Swift had obtained Harley's assurance of quick
and favourable action in regard to the remission to the Irish
clergy of the First Fruits and Twentieth Parts. It was, of
course, altogether to Harley's advantage to push this matter
through to a speedy conclusion—the sum involved was
small, the Queen was well disposed—if he could thereby
enlist the services of one whose natural gift for effective
public writing he had the acuity to recognize as unmatched
in all England. Swift's elation over the successful outcome
of his official mission was, however, short-lived, for even
as he was announcing his victory to Archbishop King, the
latter—still in ignorance of how things stood in London—
was informing him that the Irish bishops had decided that
Swift was too much of a Whig to have any influence with
the new Ministry, and that further negotiations were to be
carried on directly through Ormonde, the Lord Lieutenant.
And in the end, when the Queen's grant came to be officially —

announced in Ireland, it was the Lord Lieutenant to whom all credit went. Swift's comment in the *Journal* a year later (20 Oct. 1711) summed up his own feelings: 'I remit [the Bishops] their First-Fruits of Ingratitude, as freely as I got the other remitted to them.'

Swift's first *Examiner* appeared on Thursday, 2 November (No. 14 by the original numbering; in the reprint this became No. 13). He wrote in all thirty-two numbers, the last for which he was wholly responsible being that for 7 June 1711 (No. 45, or No. 44 in the reprint; it should be added that the issue for the following week opened with a passage by him). Swift's assignment was an all-important one, for in the absence of anything like daily newspaper reports covering the proceedings of Parliament such a journal as the *Examiner* kept the public abreast of current developments while it undertook at the same time to mould everyday opinion. Swift's weekly comments varied in tone, subject matter, and manner of approach, but they were always directed with incomparable skill at the public whom they were designed to sway. Thanks to the acumen of Harley and St. John the prince of political journalists, whose powers the Whigs could not bring themselves to acknowledge, had become the spokesman of the new Ministry.

The political situation at the moment when Swift assumed the editorship of the *Examiner* was briefly the following. The war with France—the War of the Spanish Succession—had been going on since 1702. England and her allies had won many victories under Marlborough's brilliant command, notably at Blenheim in 1704 and Ramillies in 1706, but these military achievements had not brought peace any nearer. Then, in 1709, had occurred the action at Malplaquet, and when it was learned that the victorious allies had suffered greater losses than the defeated enemy, the English public began to question openly the entire conduct of the war and the need of prolonging it. Another marked change in sentiment occurred shortly afterwards as a result of the government's prosecution of Dr. Henry Sacheverell for a High Tory sermon preached in November 1709. By the time this clergyman had been tried, found guilty by the Lords (20 March 1710), and given the lightest of punishments the country at large had been brought to a state of anger and alarm by the persistent cry of 'The Church is in danger!' The Godolphin Ministry, now associated not only with a war which had become unpopular but with what was represented as anti-Church policy, was thoroughly discredited, and Queen Anne, acting in response to public opinion and quite within her constitutional powers, proceeded through the spring and summer of 1710 to make many changes in the Council. Godolphin himself was dismissed on 8 August. A month later, when Swift arrived in London, Harley had taken office as Chancellor of the Exchequer and St. John as one of the Secretaries of State.

The new Ministry was favourable to the Church. It was committed to bringing the war to as speedy a conclusion as possible. But though it was dominantly Tory, Harley and an influential group of moderates still envisaged it as a Queen's Ministry above party. It was the overwhelming Tory victory in the elections that October that made impossible any such lofty attitude. Nevertheless, though Toryism had now triumphed, Harley himself was no hothead. He occupied a position lying somewhere between the Whigs, whose defeat he had engineered, and violent Tories of the October Club, now clamouring for extreme measures; and he still had with him a strong moderate element represented by Shrewsbury, Newcastle, and Somerset. The Church would be protected, steps would be taken to secure a peace—actually, secret negotiations looking towards an end of the war had already been opened with France—but to Harley and those who stood with him these matters of policy did not seem to be dictated by partisanship at all but by the general will of the nation. It is important to remember all this, while we are reading the

Examiner, for it was to Harley that Swift had pledged his loyalty and it was Harley's view of the political situation which served to establish his own interpretation.

In his opening numbers Swift lost no time in setting up a definite position as a base for his forthcoming operations. He was one, he informed his readers, who had generally followed the practice of conversing 'in equal Freedom with the deserving Men of both Parties'. Nothing was more wanted in England than just such a paper as this, an impartial *Examiner*, and he promised to do his best to make it what it ought to be 'without entring into the Violences of either Party'. Each faction had come to be associated with certain evils, all of which ought to be fought against: 'on one side Fanaticism and Infidelity in Religion; and Anarchy, under the Name of a Commonwealth, in Government: On the other Side, Popery, Slavery, and the Pretender from *France*'. What is the modern reader to make of such professions? Were they an artful pose on Swift's part? In his capacity of Examiner had he created still another character in order to further his rhetorical purposes? His insistence that he was a reasonable and moderate person, friendly with deserving men of both parties was of course intended to add force to his indictment of Whig policies; but at the same time it expressed his perfectly genuine view not only of his own position but of the character of Harley's Ministry. In his own mind he was neither Whig nor Tory. He spoke of himself as belonging to the Church party—the party which he had defined with such care in the *Sentiments*. As for the Ministry, it had come into being in response to the desires of all the reasonable elements in the kingdom, and it was these elements that it was now engaged in serving. Between the 'mad, ridiculous Extreams' on both sides there lay a right path 'so broad and plain, as to be easily kept' once the nation had been put into it. The Whigs might talk of a Tory faction, but to whom were they really referring? To 'the Queen and

Ministry, almost the whole Clergy, and nine Parts in ten of the Kingdom'. Swift's partisanship was real, it was intense and bitter, it was to lead him into more than one ungenerous act, it certainly involved an element of passionate self-deception. Yet despite all this, Swift's sincerity in maintaining as he always did that he spoke for the nation is beyond doubt. If there was a touch of both pedantry and naïveté in such a claim, it should not be forgotten that the concept of a Ministry above party, a concept going back to the Restoration era, still lingered on in Queen Anne's England.

With his character as an Examiner firmly established, Swift proceeded to develop his attack along several lines. Any fears which men might entertain as a result of the recent turn of events were declared to be ill-grounded. Without some such change as had just occurred it was doubtful, his readers were told, whether the constitution either in Church or State could have been long preserved, for under the Whigs the nation had been brought to the brink of ruin :

Here, has this Island of ours, for the greatest Part of twenty Years lain under the Influence of such Counsels and Persons, whose Principle and Interest it was to corrupt our Manners, blind our Understandings, drain our Wealth, and in Time destroy our Constitution both in Church and State . . .[1]

As he approached the question of the war he was again careful to manoeuvre himself into an advantageous position. Who stood to gain from a prolongation of the war? Not the nation at large, not ordinary men, not those who lived on the land, but a new species which had appeared since the Revolution, consisting of military men together with those 'whose whole Fortunes lie in Funds and Stocks'. Here was an entirely new class, a new interest—that of the moneyed men. It was they who were largely responsible

[1] *The Examiner*, Thursday, 9 Nov. 1710 (No. 14 in reprint).

for the war in the first place, and they were the only ones who were now benefiting from a continuation of hostilities.

Upon these Considerations alone, it was the most prudent Course imaginable in the QUEEN, to lay hold of the Disposition of the People for changing the Parliament and Ministry at this Juncture; and extricating her self, as soon as possible out of the Pupilage of those who found their Accounts only in perpetuating the War.[1]

Week after week through the course of that winter and the ensuing spring of 1711 the Examiner drove home his charges against those who stood in opposition to the new Ministry. The fallen party was 'patched up of heterogenous, inconsistent Parts'.[2] It harboured all those who wished for the downfall of the present Church and State—Dissenters, deists, freethinkers. Allied with the moneyed men, 'preferring, on all Occasions, the *Moneyed* Interest before the *Landed*', it had sought to keep itself in office by prolonging the war unnecessarily, and now it was bent on preventing the party in power from making peace.[3] It was also engaged in implanting in men's minds the fear that present policies were leading up to the Pretender's return, whereas in truth it was the perpetual discontent of the Whigs that was most likely to bring such a disaster to pass.[4] Though the issues which were of such passionate interest to Swift and his original readers have long since ceased to stir us one way or the other, we can scarcely remain insensible to the sheer rhetorical power displayed throughout the pages of the *Examiner*—complicated details are marshalled with incomparable skill; the presentation is always simple, persuasive; and Swift is never once off key, even his most extreme statements preserving an air of complete reasonableness.

[1] *The Examiner*, 2 Nov. 1710 (No. 13 in reprint).
[2] ibid., 5 April 1711 (No. 35 in reprint).
[3] ibid., 5 April 1711.
[4] ibid., 3 May 1711 (No. 39 in reprint).

The best-known passages are those in which Swift is falling upon Wharton and Marlborough. From the point of view of party strategy there were very good reasons for attacking both men: the Earl of Wharton, late Lord Lieutenant in Ireland, was a distinguished and powerful Whig, associated with what to Swift was the anti-Church movement, while Marlborough meant both the fallen Whig Ministry—at the end it had come to be virtually a Marlborough-Godolphin Ministry—and the policy of maintaining the war against France. However, it is impossible not to see in the attacks which Swift now directed against these two figures a deeper significance. A direct descendant of the lampooners of the Restoration, Swift had something in his literary and artistic constitution that could find expression only through the "satiric rhetoric of defamation." We should observe, though, how careful Swift was to avoid anything like intemperate diatribes in the passages directed at Wharton and Marlborough, the deadliness of the *Examiner's* accusations lying in the unbroken illusion of magisterial reasonableness. Wharton was first attacked, briefly, in the second of Swift's *Examiners* (9 Nov. 1710), where the simplicity of his genius was attributed to 'nothing else but an inexhaustible Fund of *Political Lyes*'. But there was far worse in store for this Whig grandee, and in the *Examiner* of 30 November Swift found occasion for one of the most effective of all his diatribes. Likening Wharton, recently Lord Lieutenant in Ireland, to Verres, the Roman governor of Sicily attacked by Cicero in his famous series of orations, the Examiner now delivered his own Oration against Verres, where occurred such passages as these:

I have brought here a Man before you, my Lords, who is a Robber of the Publick Treasure; an Overturner of Law and Justice; and the Disgrace, as well as Destruction of the *Sicilian* Province . . .

. . . what Eloquence will be able to defend a Man, whose Life hath been tainted with so many scandalous Vices, and who hath been so long condemned by the universal Opinion of the World? To pass over the foul Stains and Ignominy of his Youth; his corrupt Management in all Employments he hath born; his Treachery and Irreligion; his Injustice and Oppression: He hath left of late such Monuments of his Villanies in *Sicily*; made such Havock and Confusion there, during his Government, that the Province cannot by any Means be restored to its former State, and hardly recover it self at all under many Years, and by a long Succession of good Governors . . .

Meanwhile an entire issue (23 Nov. 1710) had been devoted to Marlborough. Was it feared that the recent changes at Court would give uneasiness to this general? Why this great clamour against what was being represented as national ingratitude to the Duke? The Examiner proceeded to compare, in terms of cold cash, England's ingratitude and what Rome had customarily bestowed on one of her victorious generals. The bill of Roman gratitude, consisting of ten separate items—one being a crown of laurel costing twopence!—was shown to have amounted to precisely £994 11s. 10d.; the bill of British ingratitude came to £540,000. Here, I believe, is the earliest use on Swift's part of the kind of arithmetical hocus-pocus that he was later to employ with such sensational effect in both the *Drapier's Letters* and the *Modest Proposal*. If it is unnecessary to defend Swift against the humourless accusation that he played fast and loose with figures, it may still be pointed out that in all these instances there is involved, in addition to the wit and exuberance, a touch of irony of the proper Swiftian quality. The item of a crown of laurel at twopence ought to put us on the right track. A situation—here a historical one—has been created with mock verisimilitude, and all the details down to the seemingly least significant are there merely awaiting direct transcription. Whether a dramatic character is brought into play or not, an effect is established which is akin to irony.

One further passage from the *Examiner*, also directed

against Marlborough, may be noted. The famous Letter to Crassus (8 Feb. 1711) shares first honours with the earlier Oration against Verres. 'I have sometimes thought,' wrote the Examiner,

that if I had lived at *Rome* in the Time of the first *Triumvirate*, I should have been tempted to write a Letter, as from an unknown Hand, to those three great Men, who had then usurped the Sovereign Power; wherein I would freely and sincerely tell each of them that Fault which I conceived was most odious, and of worst Consequence to the Commonwealth; That, to *Crassus*, should have been sent to him after his Conquests in *Mesopotamia*, and in the following Terms.

In the Letter thus introduced the charge of avarice is pressed against Marlborough with an eloquence the more effective because of the restraint which the writer, with Roman dignity, feels compelled to exercise.

It may be noted in passing that Swift found no place in the *Examiner* for the most severe of the personal attacks launched during these months, the *Short Character of His Excellency Thomas Earl of Wharton* (about Dec. 1710, though dated 30 Aug. 1710). In reading this we are reminded once more that Swift's roots lay in the Restoration era, for it was then that the prose *character* had been turned from a study of general characteristics into a lethal rhetorical weapon for use against one's enemies. The tone of Swift's *Character* is fairly represented by this curt description of Wharton's religious affiliations: 'He is a Presbyterian in Politics, and an Atheist in Religion; but he chuseth at present to whore with a Papist.' This is incomparable in its way, but Swift knew that it did not accord with the carefully established tone of the *Examiner*. The appearance of the *Character* as a separate publication tells us much about Swift's conscious craftsmanship.

When Swift withdrew from the *Examiner* in June 1711 the national scene had in certain respects changed. That spring England had received from France an open request for peace. As a matter of fact, secret conversations between the two powers had been in progress since the previous August, but it was now felt that the time had come to bring these negotiations into the open, and it was at this point that St. John assumed control at the English end. During the summer of 1711 the representatives of the two nations reached agreement on a number of terms as between themselves, but England's allies had not as yet been brought in for consultation and a peace would have to await a conference of the Powers, due to get under way early in 1712. In the meantime St. John had succeeded in obtaining numerous commercial advantages for the English, and preliminary articles between France and England were signed in London that October. The great question was now whether Parliament, scheduled to meet before Christmas, would approve the further steps necessary to make peace an actuality. The Whigs were opposed; an attempt was being made to set Harley and St. John against one another on this issue; and certain moderates like Shrewsbury were visibly uneasy over St. John's treatment of the other allies. It was a most critical moment for the Ministry.

Swift published two pamphlets in the early autumn of 1711: *Some Remarks upon a Pamphlet entitled A Letter to the Seven Lords* (18 Aug.) and *A New Journey to Paris* (11 Sept.). Both have a political background, but it is the *New Journey to Paris* that is directly connected with the public events just referred to. Matthew Prior had been secretly sent over to Paris that summer to carry on personal negotiations with Torcy, Louis's Minister, but on his return home his mission had come to light when he was arrested by a too-suspicious officer of the custom house. Swift's *New Journey*, described to Stella as 'a formal grave lie, from the beginning to the end', was in its way another tale of a tub, designed to distract the town's attention while peace terms were being made ready behind the scenes. The pamphlet is unusually interesting from the literary

point of view, for besides offering a prime example of the
created character within the imaginary situation it marks
what is really the first appearance of Lemuel Gulliver,
though as yet he is only the humble Frenchman, the supposed author of the *New Journey*, who we are to believe
has served Prior as a servant and is now giving an account
of his master's recent journey from Calais to Paris and
back. Though this writer signs himself the Sieur du
Baudrier and does his best to represent himself as attending Prior in the capacity of a secretary, we are warned by
the 'translator' that he is only a menial servant giving himself airs with true French vanity. From du Baudrier's
account we see that while he was accompanying Prior during that gentleman's travels he was made aware for the first
time in his life of comparative national values. Here was
France in all its scarcity and poverty, here an English
traveller who had the effrontery to pretend that his own
island had felt no effects like these upon trade or agriculture.
Gulliver's national pride was to be aroused by the King of
Brobdingnag's slighting remarks on Europe; conversing
with his English employer, the Sieur du Baudrier was stung
into holding forth on the superiority of things in France:

I made bold to return for Answer, That in our Nation we only
consulted the Magnificence and Power of our Prince; but that in
England, as I was informed, the Wealth of the Kingdom was so
divided among the People, that little or nothing was left to their
Sovereign; . . . That I hoped, when he went to *Versailles*, he would
allow the Grandeur of our Potent Monarch to exceed . . . any other
in *Europe*, by which he would find that what he called the Poverty
of our Nation, was rather the Effect of Policy in our Court, than
any real Want or Necessity. Monsieur *Prior* had no better Answer
to make me, than that he was no Stranger to our Court, the Splendor
of our Prince, and the Maxims by which he governed; but for his
part, he thought those Countries were happier, when the Productions
of it were more equally divided: Such unaccountable Notions is the
Prejudice of Education apt to give! . . .

The closing incident, which finds Prior and the writer accosted by a group of poor people in a small village, seems also to look forward to scenes in *Gulliver's Travels*.

But it was not to write short pamphlets like these that Swift had given up the editorship of the *Examiner*. Harley and St. John, looking ahead to the approaching session of Parliament and the stormy debates which were bound to arise over the question of peace, had decided to entrust to Swift the important and difficult task of preparing a sort of handbook which would sum matters up from the Ministry's point of view and present the arguments for peace as succinctly and clearly as possible. From the summer of 1711 on into the autumn Swift was in close touch with the two ministers, going down to Windsor with them on many occasions. The pamphlet was finished on 24 November and came out three days later. *The Conduct of the Allies* is one of the masterpieces of political journalism. It sold tremendously—in two months six editions, amounting to something like 11,000 copies, had been printed. 'The Tory lords and commons in parliament argue all from it,' he wrote to Stella; 'and all agree, that never any thing of that kind was of so great consequence, or made so many converts.'[1] That it is no longer of much interest to the present-day reader is really owing to Swift's unfailing instinct for the tone and approach best suited to the immediate purpose. This was no occasion for the kind of writing which he had sometimes permitted himself in the *Examiner*. Here there must be a studied avoidance of anything having the appearance of rhetoric; the reader was to feel only the weight of facts:

. . . I presume it will appear, by plain Matters of Fact, that no Nation was ever so long or so scandalously abused by the Folly, the Temerity, the Corruption, the Ambition of its domestick Enemies; or treated with so much Insolence, Injustice and Ingratitude by its foreign friends.

[1] *Journal to Stella*, 18 Dec. 1711.

The Marlborough family, Godolphin, allied to it by marriage, and the moneyed men had between them put England into the war and kept her there.

... what have we been Fighting for all this while? The Answer is ready; We have been Fighting for the Ruin of the Publick Interest, and the Advancement of a Private. We have been fighting to raise the Wealth and Grandeur of a particular Family; to enrich Usurers and Stock-jobbers; and to cultivate the pernicious Designs of a Faction, by destroying the Landed-Interest. The Nation begins now to think these *Blessings* not worth Fighting for any longer, and therefore desires a Peace.

The month of December 1711 was one of crisis. Parliament reassembled, and as a result of the Tory Earl of Nottingham's desertion to the Whigs in the matter of peace, an anti-ministerial vote was carried in the House of Lords. With the Tories holding a majority in the lower House a situation developed which caused general concern, but at the last moment the creation of twelve new Tory peers allowed the Ministry to break through this impasse. Swift received news of this dramatic stroke on the evening of 29 December and tore open his letter to Stella in order to add a jubilant postscript announcing the Tory victory. The last day of the year saw Marlborough dismissed from his offices. The Ministry had triumphed completely, and the policies which Swift had championed so brilliantly were assured of parliamentary support.

Throughout this course of events Swift had been in a state of great excitement and irritability. Characteristically he found relief in lampooning those who had come to symbolize the enemy. Nottingham (generally known as 'Dismal'), who had voted with the Whigs, was derided in *An Excellent New Song, Being the Intended Speech of a famous Orator against Peace* (6 Dec.). The Duchess of Somerset, close to the Queen and sharing all of her husband's Whig sympathies, was excoriated in the unforgivable verses of the *Windsor Prophecy* (24 Dec.). At the moment of his final humiliation Marlborough was attacked in the *Fable of the Widow and her Cat* (Jan. 1712 ; some doubt, however, still remains as to Swift's authorship), and a few weeks later in the *Fable of Midas* (14 Feb.). Indefensible as Swift's conduct appears to us, it must be taken as typical of several generations of writers for whom the pasquinade was an established weapon. *Tempora mutantur.*

Following upon the Tory victory of the closing days of 1711 there came a long period during which the Allied Powers and France, meeting at Utrecht, wrangled over peace terms. The situation was a complicated one, for in consequence of St. John's manoeuvring he and the French representatives had already come to an understanding on many points, with the result that before the Allies could present a united front to France, England was obliged to bring the Dutch and the Austrians into line. To do this extreme measures were necessary, and in July 1712 England withdrew from military operations and arranged a temporary truce with France, leaving the other allies to learn how weak they were without English support. Thereupon the Dutch gave in. Previously, in 1709, England and Holland had signed what was known as the Barrier Treaty, by which England had agreed that as an indispensable condition of any peace which might be arranged the Dutch should be given an effective barrier against France in the form of a line of towns and fortifications along the French frontier. Since coming to power the Tories had made a great deal of the unnecessarily generous terms which the Whig Ministry, who had negotiated the Barrier Treaty, had consented to grant the Dutch. A new Treaty between England and Holland, in which the barrier was materially reduced in extent, was agreed upon early in 1713, and on the last day of March the war which had been in progress since 1702 came to an end with the signing of the Treaties of Utrecht. News of the latter event reached London three days later, and when Parliament reassembled on 9 April the Queen made the formal announcement in her speech to both Houses. Oxford had shown Swift parts of this speech some days before, and Swift told Stella how he had then corrected it 'in sevrall Places'. He had at the same time, he further observed, 'penned the vote of Address of thanks for the Speech'—i.e. the Lords' *Address*, which was printed two days after the opening of Parliament.

Though nothing that Swift did in the way of political writing during 1712 and the early months of 1713 was comparable in importance to the *Examiner* and the *Conduct of the Allies*, several of the pamphlets of this period make surprisingly good reading today and all bear witness to Swift's unfailing resourcefulness as a controversialist. *Some Advice to the Members of the October Club*, which appeared in the latter part of January 1712, was his first prose publication after the *Conduct of the Allies*. It is in the form of a Letter from a Person of Honour and is addressed to the Tory extremists who were demanding that the Ministry abandon its moderate course by turning out all the Whigs and making a '*thorough Change*', with respect to Employments'. Swift's purpose was to protect the Ministry against this sort of pressure, the results of which could be disastrous at a time when nothing should be allowed to interfere with the negotiations for peace; and accordingly he had his Person of Honour address the Tory zealots in a tone best calculated to give them pause. In February came *Some Remarks on the Barrier Treaty*, announced as being by the author of the *Conduct of the Allies* and in effect a short supplement to that famous tract. The original Barrier Treaty of 1709 was about to be debated in the House of Commons, and this pamphlet placed the text of the Treaty before the public and at the same time sought to cast an unfavourable light on the Dutch. More impressive than either of these is the *Letter to a Whig Lord* (July). Like the *Advice to the October Club* it was intended to strengthen the Ministry's position during the drive for peace, but was addressed to moderate Whigs instead of Tory extremists. Here Swift's middle style is seen at its most impressive, as in the notable paragraph with which the *Letter* ends:

I shall conclude, my Lord, with putting you in mind, that you are a Subject of the Queen, a Peer of the Realm, and a Servant of your Country; and in any of these Capacities, you are not to consider what you dislike, in the Persons of those who are in the Administration, but the manner of conducting themselves while they are in. And then I do not despair, but your own good Sense will fully convince you, that the Prerogative of your Prince, without which Her Government cannot subsist; the Honour of your House, which hath been always the great Asserter of that Prerogative; and the Welfare of your Country, are too precious to be made a Sacrifice to the Malice, the Interest, and the Ambition of a few Party-Leaders.

The events of July 1712 brought from Swift a burst of activity. One of the conditions upon which England had, at the beginning of July, entered into a temporary truce with the French was that Dunkirk should be occupied by British troops; and until General Hill took possession a few days later, there was a certain amount of concern lest some untoward incident arise, and the Whigs chose to remain highly suspicious of the entire matter even after the French port had been taken over. The Dunkirk affair raised a storm of pamphlets, to which Swift contributed his share. Furthermore, a new Licensing Act, which placed a tax on newspapers of the half- and whole-sheet size with a view to the suppression of libels, was due to come into effect at the beginning of August, and in anticipation of this Swift saw to the publication of a number of penny papers. All of the things which he printed at this time have not been recovered, but among those which we now possess there are two items which take their place among the liveliest and most arresting things that Swift produced during his career as Tory journalist. One, a short pamphlet, is the *Letter of Thanks from my Lord Wharton to the Lord Bp of S. Asaph*; the other is a half-sheet paper entitled *A Hue and Cry after Dismal* (both in July 1712). Fleetwood, Bishop of St. Asaph, had recently pleased the Whigs mightily by his remarks in a Preface appearing in a new edition of some of his sermons. Swift's *Letter* is ridicule of the double-edged kind that he knew so well how to devise. The writer is Wharton, who is taking this opportunity to express his admiration of the noteworthy passages in the Bishop's sermons and to thank that divine for his eminent services to all Whigs and atheists. Fleetwood's compassion at the destruction of a well-known dissenting chapel in London during the Sacheverell riots draws from Wharton the following reminiscence:

The generous Compassion your Lordship has shewn upon this tragical Occasion, makes me believe your Lordship will not be unaffected with an Accident that had like to have befallen a poor Whore of my Acquaintance about that Time, who being big with Whig, was so alarmed at the Rising of the Mob, that she had like to have miscarried upon it; for the Logical Jade presently concluded, (and the Inference was natural enough) that if they began with pulling down Meeting-houses, it might end in demolishing those Houses of Pleasure, where she constantly paid her Devotion; and, indeed, there seems a close Connexion between *Extempore* Prayer and *Extempore* Love.

The *Hue and Cry after Dismal* was sheer mischief. Dunkirk having now been occupied contrary to all the dark forebodings of the Whigs, did they not deserve to be made sport of? Could there be any harm in suggesting that they had hoped that Dunkirk would not be occupied? And if that was what had been in their hearts, why should they not have plotted to keep the English troops out by inciting the French to armed resistance? In this case, they would have had to send some agent to the spot. Why not Dismal, the Earl of Nottingham, who had served the Whigs so well before? Any logical person, jade or otherwise, could follow all this by natural inference. Swift's account of what befell the Earl after he had disguised himself as a chimney-sweeper and ventured into Dunkirk with brooms and poles and a bunch of holly upon his shoulders is first-rate narration, fictional in every sense.

There remains to be mentioned one further work produced during this period of long-drawn-out negotiations at Utrecht. It was in September 1712 that Swift began a detailed historical account of the Ministry's efforts in behalf of peace. In his own mind this was to be quite as important a work as the *Examiner* and the *Conduct of the Allies*, and he thought to finish it and have it published in time to be of service to the Ministry in case they came under attack for their conduct of the negotiations. But as things turned out, Swift encountered all sorts of difficulties: his friends in the Ministry were negligent in giving him necessary help; some thought his account 'too dangerous to publish'; and Sir Thomas Hanmer, to whom he lent his manuscript, kept it three months. By the time he finished his work in the middle of May 1713 the immediate occasion for which he had been preparing it had passed, Parliament having already received the Queen's formal announcement of peace. Years later, when Swift again tried to arrange for the publication of his history, there were those who still advised against its appearance. Thus it came about that the work known as the *History of the Four Last Years of the Queen* remained in manuscript until 1758. When taken along with the two short pieces which Swift wrote subsequent to the Queen's death—the *Memoirs Relating to that Change in the Queen's Ministry* and the *Enquiry into the Behaviour of the Queen's Last Ministry* (both printed in 1765)—it gives a record of the highest historical importance of the events leading up to the Treaty of Utrecht.

It was in April 1713 that Swift finally came into his reward. He stayed on in London for some weeks—it was then that he finished the *History of the Four Last Years of the Queen*—but on 1 June he set out for Ireland and on the 13th he was installed Dean of St. Patrick's. He believed that his services to the Ministry were at an end, but it was not long before he began to receive messages from London urging his speedy return. The long-standing quarrel between Oxford and Bolingbroke was reaching a point of new intensity, and it was apparent to everyone that the Ministry was in immediate danger of falling apart. Those closest to the people concerned were in agreement that if anyone could bring about a reconciliation it was Swift. He was back in London by 9 September. The concluding chapter of his career as a journalist working in behalf of the Oxford Ministry covers the period extending down to the Queen's death (1 Aug. 1713) and his departure for Ireland (16 Aug.). The Whig opposition was still harping on Dunkirk, maintaining that the terms calling for the demolition of the city's fortifications and the destruction of its harbour were not being carried out. But a matter of much deeper concern was that of the succession, for it was increasingly apparent that the Queen's days were numbered, and all sorts of rumours were circulating regarding the Pretender. Steele now took it upon himself to sound a general alarm, his *Importance of Dunkirk Consider'd* appearing about two weeks after Swift's return to London, *The Crisis*—which had been advertised since October—about the middle of January 1714. Both of these Swift answered. He replied to Steele's charges regarding Dunkirk in the pamphlet entitled *The Importance of the Guardian Considered* (about 31 Oct.), and to the *Crisis* in *The Public Spirit of the Whigs* (23 Feb. 1714). By spring it was clear to Swift that nothing could any longer bring Oxford and Bolingbroke together, and he decided, wisely enough, to leave London and go into retirement in Berkshire. *Some Free Thoughts upon the Present State of Affairs* (printed in 1741) was apparently begun before his departure from London at the end of May but finished at Letcombe; *Some Considerations upon the Consequences hoped and feared from the Death of the Queen* (printed in 1765) was also begun at Letcombe but never brought to a conclusion. Of the writings of this final period, *Some Free Thoughts* is perhaps the most interesting to the general reader today. Swift is here asserting once again the belief he had voiced so often in the preceding years—that Oxford's Ministry had from the first enjoyed the confidence of the vast majority of the nation. Why, then, had it come to ruin? From 'the want of a due Communication and Concert', he answers, and from a refusal ever to take the direct and obvious line of procedure. Nowhere has Swift expressed more clearly and simply his contempt for unnecessary subtlety—'this reserved mysterious way of acting'—and his faith in common sense. The reasonable part of mankind will never be convinced, he writes,

> that the most plain, short, easy, safe, and lawfull Way to any good End, is not more eligible, than one directly contrary in some or all of these Qualities . . . God hath given the Bulk of Mankind a Capacity to understand Reason when it is fairly offered; and by Reason they would easily be governed, if it were left to their Choice.

Referring to the fear that the Hanoverian Succession had been placed in danger, Swift argues at length that all the circumstances go to prove such a fear to be groundless:

> From all these Considerations I must therefore lay it down as an uncontestible Truth, that the Succession to these Kingdoms in the Illustrious House of Hannover is as firmly secured as the Nature of the Thing can possibly admit . . .

When Swift's career as a Tory journalist is reviewed from a modern point of view, certain things stand forth. It is true that he remained in ignorance of the communications which Oxford and Bolingbroke held with the Pretender, but this does not mean that his relations with the Ministry were not close. He was not in a position to see everything, but in regard to the broad ministerial policy and the negotiations leading up to peace there were not many others who had as full a knowledge of the facts, and it is this that gives historical importance to so much of his writing of the 1710-1714 period. As for his evaluation of events, it would appear that he was not so much in error as has sometimes been assumed. The Oxford Ministry was not one above party, but Swift's representation of it as moderate in its purposes was largely in accord with the facts. And finally, we should do well to bear in mind while reading Swift's tracts that the peace which Bolingbroke and his colleagues designed was, everything considered, one of the notable achievements of modern diplomacy and statesmanship. The *Examiner*, the *Conduct of the Allies*, and the *History of the Four Last Years of the Queen* are to be associated with no mean cause. More could be said about the historical aspects of Swift's journalistic work, but though such aspects are important they are not, after all, what continues to attract the reader of Swift. What impresses one is the writing itself, from the arrangement of the material down to small details of phrasing. Swift was never more of a master of English prose than in these contributions to the party press.

Though the non-controversial prose and verse of the years here under review are not part of the record of Swift's journalistic activities, they can scarcely be dismissed with no notice whatever.

One of the first things which he composed after his arrival in London in the autumn of 1710 was the paper which appeared in the *Tatler* for 28 September (No. 230). It is concerned with one of Swift's favourite topics, 'the corruption of style and writing', and in the best manner of the *Tatler* combines wit and didactic purpose. The writer, having presented a copy of a letter recently received from a person most accomplished in all the corruptions which have recently crept into the language, uses this to call attention to the worst features of present-day style. He ends by expressing the hope that the *Tatler*—or, more properly, Isaac Bickerstaff—may be 'the Instrument of introducing into our Style, that Simplicity which is the best and truest Ornament of most Things in human Life.'

Shortly after the appearance of this *Tatler* Swift noted in the *Journal* (10 Oct.) that he was at work on another contribution for Steele, 'my poetical *Description of a Shower in London*'. The *Description of a City Shower* appeared on 17 October (*Tatler* No. 238), and Swift promptly reported on its success to Stella. He had every reason to be proud of it, for he had created out of the materials of parody and anti-poetic realism an enduring *genre* piece. The concluding paragraph is remarkable for its language and its wonderful energy, both typical of a realism which in the eighteenth century was so often defiance of all the polite traditions :

> Now from all Parts the swelling Kennels flow,
> And bear their Trophies with them as they go :
> Filth of all Hues and Odours seem to tell
> What Street they sail'd from, by their Sight and Smell.
> They, as each Torrent drives, with rapid Force
> From *Smithfield*, or *St. Pulchre's* shape their Course,
> And in huge Confluent join at *Snow-Hill* Ridge,
> Fall from the *Conduit* prone to *Holborn-Bridge*.
> Sweepings from Butchers Stalls, Dung, Guts, and Blood,
> Drown'd Puppies, stinking Sprats, all drench'd in Mud,
> Dead Cats and Turnip-Tops come tumbling
>   down the Flood.

The year 1711, largely taken up with the *Examiner* and the *Conduct of the Allies*, brought from Swift comparatively little in the way of non-political writing, though it did see the publication of his *Miscellanies in Prose and Verse* (end of Feb. 1711), where with the exception of the *Tale of a Tub* and the two shorter satires associated with it most of his work up to that point was now brought together, some of the items being printed for the first time. Though Swift protested to Stella that he knew nothing of the affair, the volume having been put out without his knowledge or consent, he had unquestionably co-operated fully with the publisher—perhaps one should put it more strongly and say that the publisher had co-operated with Swift—and the appearance of this collection was an event of major importance in his literary career.

May of the following year saw the publication of the only thing which Swift ever allowed to appear over his name—*A Proposal for Correcting, Improving and Ascertaining the English Tongue; In a Letter To the . . . Lord High Treasurer . . .* Swift was here returning to the subject which he had briefly touched upon in his Letter to the *Tatler* a year and a half earlier. Our language is extremely imperfect, we are told, and is suffering corruption day by day, yet there is no necessity why it should be perpetually changing. Swift goes on to propose to Oxford the establishment of a body comparable to the French Academy which might determine some way of 'ascertaining and fixing our language for ever, after such alterations are made in it as shall be thought requisite'. Of all the Proposals, serious or ironic, which came from Swift's pen, this is the one which is perhaps least likely to be received sympathetically today. We may well feel that on this subject Dr. Johnson was wiser than Dr. Swift: 'I am not yet so lost in lexicography as to forget that "words are the daughters of earth, and that things are the sons of heaven". Language is only the instrument of science, and words are but the signs of ideas.' But it is unfair to hold Swift too strictly accountable for views which were thoroughly characteristic of the earlier prescriptive grammarians of the century. And if we still protest that blindness to viability in language is blindness to viability in all human experience, we can only remind ourselves of Swift's theory of prudence: by observing the historical past, we learn how to slow down the operation of those natural forces which in changing our civilization bring it closer to its ultimate corruption.

In the last prose work that need be mentioned here Swift was again on the attack and again using as his weapon the broadest of irony. Anthony Collins had just published his deistical *Discourse on Freethinking*. This Swift turned inside out in his well-known parody, *Mr. C—ne's Discourse of Free-Thinking, Put into plain English, by way of Abstract, For the Use of the Poor. By a Friend of the Author* (25 Jan. 1713). Though the satire is directly concerned with deism it is not without a political note, for Swift could not resist bringing the deists into association with the Whigs.

Of the later poems of this period there are at least three which deserve special notice, and in all of them Swift is found writing of himself and his own experiences. *Part of the Seventh Epistle of the First Book of Horace Imitated* was written and published in 1713, after he had returned to England in answer to the entreaties of his friends. It is addressed to Oxford and purports to give the story of how the author and 'Harley, the Nation's great Support', had first met, of Swift's appointment to the Deanery of St. Patrick's and his departure for Ireland, and of his subsequent return to England, poverty-stricken as a result of expenses incurred in assuming his new station. *The Author Upon Himself* and the imitation, *Horace, Part of the Sixth Satire of the Second Book*, were both written at Letcombe during his closing days in England. The first gives a vivid account of how those whom he had variously offended had sought his undoing:

> By an [old red hair'd, murd'ring Hag] pursu'd,
> A Crazy Prelate, and a Royal Prude.
> By dull Divines, who look with
>   envious Eyes,
> On ev'ry Genius that attempts to rise;
> And pausing o'er a Pipe, with doubtful Nod,
> Gives Hints, that Poets ne'er believe in God.
> So, Clowns on Scholars as on Wizards look,
> And take a Folio for a conj'ring Book.

Thus for the Duchess of Somerset, the Archbishop of York, Queen Anne, and those of his clerical brethren who suspected him for his wit. The *Imitation* is a reminiscence of his experiences while close to the Ministry. Its quiet tone —a contrast to that of *The Author Upon Himself*—was in reality not an expression of peacefulness but of bitter nostalgia and a dread of what was then impending.

VI

IRISH PATRIOT

OF the various public *rôles* assumed by Swift at one time or another that of Irish patriot unquestionably holds the strongest appeal today. As the Drapier Dean, fierce opponent not only of the relatively obscure William Wood but of Walpole himself and the English Ministry, he exhibited a resolution and an energy which touch our imagination as does nothing else in his entire career. There is much in Swift that is uncongenial to the modern temper—his view of man and of western history, and his theory of society, stressing containment and a rigid preservation of the *status quo*. But in the Irish public figure these negative qualities—or what we regard as such—take on another aspect. If at other times and in other *rôles* Swift seems to be laying the dead hand of conformity upon so much that is vital in human experience, the great protagonist of Irish independence creates a quite different atmosphere. He lives by action; it is action that he is urging upon his fellow countrymen.

Queen Anne had died on 1 August 1714 and by the 24th Swift was back in Dublin. Each day that passed made clearer the utter defeat of the Tory party and the sort of retribution which was likely to be demanded by their triumphant opponents. The English colony in Ireland, Whig to the core, rejoiced at the change brought on by the Queen's death, and turned in savage scorn upon those of its members known to be Tory sympathizers. Even if Swift had had the desire and the psychic strength for open warfare here in Dublin, he could have made no headway against such overwhelming opposition. As it was he found himself in no mood for any sort of struggle. The weeks of suspense preceding the Queen's death, the despair felt while watching the steady disintegration of Oxford's Ministry, and a sense of final catastrophe had brought him close to utter exhaustion. St. Patrick's had become a refuge from a world turned upside down. Such writing as he did was concerned, as had been the two historical pieces he had worked on during his last months in England, with the conduct of affairs on the part of the late Ministry. *Memoirs, Relating to That Change Which Happened in the Queen's Ministry in the year 1710* (not printed until 1765) is dated October 1714 and was designed to parallel and supplement his *History of the Four Last Years*. The ensuing year brought to Swift a sense of personal danger as news from England told of the impeachment of Oxford, Bolingbroke, and Ormonde. The two latter fled to the continent; Oxford, who stood his ground, was imprisoned in the Tower in July 1715. Earlier, Swift had been warned to hide his papers, and that May a letter to him from the Duke of Ormonde and another from his printer, John Barber, were seized by the Irish authorities. Steadfast in his loyalty to Oxford, utterly incredulous of the charges now being raised against the former minister, but conscious that he could extend to him only such aid as lay in the power of the historian, he now undertook still another account of the course of events during the latter part of Anne's reign, and in June wrote the first chapter of what he called an *Enquiry into the Behaviour of the Queen's Last Ministry* (finished in 1720; revised thereafter; printed in 1765). It was to this *Enquiry* that he was referring in his letter of 19 July to Oxford, in which he remarked that he had taken care that the Earl should be properly represented to posterity 'in spite of all the rage and malice of your enemies'. Two years were to pass before Oxford's trial and acquittal, during which period he continued to be confined in the Tower. The varied emotions experienced by Swift as he brooded over the treatment of one whom he regarded as a true patriot found expression in that Imitation of Horace which he composed in 1716, *To the Earl of Oxford . . . Sent to him when he was in the Tower, before his Tryal.*

Living in this manner in the past, Swift knew and cared nothing about the new age in politics beyond what affected the lives of his distinguished friends. To Irish affairs outside his own realm of St. Patrick's he was completely indifferent, and for several years he made no effort to enlarge the small circle of friends who had greeted him on his return from England. Gradually, however, his energies had been returning. He had begun to form new friendships, the most important being those with Sheridan and Delany. Late in 1719 he had confided to Charles Ford that politics were again raising his passions. But the surest sign that the long period of apathy was coming to an end was to be seen in his returning interest in verse, evidenced by three poems of unusual power written in 1719-20—*Phillis, or, The Progress of Love*; *The Progress of Beauty*; and *The Progress of Poetry.* By this time all of Swift's literary powers were fully awake, and by 1721 he had begun work on *Gulliver's Travels.*

It should not be forgotten that Swift's interest in the affairs and problems of Ireland antedated by many years the period we are about to consider. As a Whig, his views had reflected his concern for the situation in Ireland, and both then and at a later time when he was close to the Tory administration he had worked for the advancement of the Irish Church. Now that he was Dean of St. Patrick's and an Irishman for good and all, he would almost certainly have found occasion sooner or later to drop the mask he had been wearing, come out of his retirement, and assume a position of leadership in the society and country to which he belonged by birth and long association. His war against the halfpence was partly revenge upon Walpole and the Whigs, but it would never have been undertaken if his

patriotism had not been thoroughly aroused. We are to
observe, too, how a few fundamental principles underlay
all his thinking, his public acts, and his writing as an Irish
statesman. These principles were nothing new. They had,
indeed, become almost a part of him since the time when,
as a younger man, he had ordered his ideas on such subjects as the nature of the community and the state, rational
liberty, and the obligations of the free citizen. Swift's view
of the ideal community is set forth in simplest terms in his
sermon *On Mutual Subjection* (precisely when it was preached
cannot be determined; it was printed in 1744). Those
familiar with the sermon literature of the Church of the
Restoration and earlier eighteenth century will recognize
in this discourse of Swift's much that is perfectly traditional.
There is insistence upon the whole and integrated community; there is the theory of social orders, every man
having his recognized place and obligated to acknowledge
his subordination to those above him. The perpetuation of
an ordered society requires the disciplined acceptance of all
this. Yet God is not a respecter of persons, nor are power,
wealth, and similar outward advantages 'Marks of God's
approving or preferring those on whom they are bestowed';
in the end we come to realize that we are all mutually
dependent on one another:

. . . the Subject must obey his Prince, because God commands it,
human Laws require it, and the Safety of the Publick maketh it
necessary . . . On the other Side, in those Countries that pretend
to Freedom, Princes are subject to those Laws which their People
have chosen; they are bound to protect their Subjects in Liberty,
Property, and Religion; to receive their Petitions, and redress their
Grievances: So, that the best Prince is, in the Opinion of wise Men,
only the greatest Servant of the Nation; not only a Servant to the
Publick in general, but in some sort to every Man in it. In the like
manner, a Servant owes Obedience, and Diligence, and Faithfulness
to his Master, from whom at the same time he hath a just Demand
for Protection, and Maintenance, and gentle Treatment. Nay, even

the poor Beggar hath a just Demand of an Alms from the Rich Man, who is guilty of Fraud, Injustice, and Oppression, if he doth not afford Relief according to his Abilities.

Despite the element of Whig political philosophy that is present here, this statement is in most respects quite in line with representative Anglican thought, which from the Restoration onwards was really more concerned with social order in and for itself than with the details of constitutional theory, and which continued to think in terms of social status, not so much by way of conscious resistance to the theories of contractualism being fostered by an emergent middle-class civilization as by force of habit and tradition. It is this tradition, rather than anything peculiar to Swift, which is present in his concept of the good society. His theory of rational freedom he had long since expressed in the fullest manner in the pamphlets of his Whig period. It only remained for him to apply this theory to those who, in his view, constituted the Irish nation. His audacity lay in doing just this. So long as Irishmen were prevented by laws passed in England from conducting their own affairs as they saw fit and controlling their own economy without interference, they did not enjoy the free citizenship which was their birthright. It was at this constitutional level that Swift planned and carried through his entire campaign as an Irish patriot. What he overlooked is, to be sure, amazing to us today, for the native Irish were wholly excluded from his community of free men, and of the Anglo-Irish only those conforming to the Established Church had full rights. He could not acknowledge and perhaps did not perceive that the restrictions on the political and economic life of Ireland were as much as anything the price exacted by England for affording protection to a colony, a garrison, stationed amongst a hostile people. The situation was as paradoxical a one as any which he ever created in his satires. Yet his achievement was great, and despite the presuppositions of his age and his class which narrowed his vision the concept of freedom which he set forth stands in the great tradition.

The appearance in May 1720 of the short pamphlet entitled *A Proposal For the Universal Use of Irish Manufacture* was the first clear evidence that the Dean of St. Patrick's had now determined to take part in the contemporary affairs of his country. His decision to do so had probably been hastened by the passage in England that March of the 'Act for the better securing the Dependency of the Kingdom of Ireland upon the Crown of Great Britain'. Swift was by no means the first Irishman to protest against the long-standing doctrine of political dependency. In 1698 William Molyneux had declared in a famous pamphlet— *The Case of Ireland's Being Bound by Acts of Parliament in England, Stated*—that Ireland was not to be looked upon as a colony. Least of all did Swift stand alone as a writer on Irish economic matters. The air was full of pamphlets, letters, projects, proposals, all designed to throw light on the economic woes of the nation and advancing all manner of schemes. Ireland's plight was very real. After the Restoration she had, it is true, enjoyed a period of considerable prosperity, but the combined force of the various Navigation Acts passed in England from 1663 onwards, the Cattle Acts of 1665 and 1680, and the legislation at the very end of the century regulating the woollen industry had now reduced the country as a whole to a state of wretched poverty, and, perhaps worst of all, had destroyed the initiative and resourcefulness of the people. All of this had been done, it must be remembered, in accordance with the accepted principles of mercantilism, which placed the prosperity of the mother country before that of her colonies, and defined prosperity as an excess of exports over imports. It followed that Ireland, like the colonies across the Atlantic, was to be prevented from engaging in such economic transactions with England as would endanger the latter's so-called favourable balance of trade. Then the Cattle Acts had stopped the importation to England of Irish cattle and meat, and the laws passed in 1698 and 1699 had prohibited the export of Irish wool and woollen goods to any country save England. Yet neither Swift nor his fellow-writers in Ireland were calling in question the point of view or the basic assumptions given by the mercantilism of their age.[1] This is not surprising, since it would have been difficult for anyone in the 1720s to know where to turn had it occurred to him to challenge standard views : the medieval theory calling for the control of all secular enterprise on religious-ascetic grounds held little appeal for the English —or, for that matter, the Anglican—mind of this period, while the doctrines of *laissez-faire*, which were eventually to supplant those of mercantilism, had not as yet been formulated, Adam Smith's *Wealth of Nations* lying half a century in the future. Swift was not taking issue with the mercantilist philosophy which had directed England's policy towards Ireland but with the principle which had just been reaffirmed in the Act of 1720. Ireland, he declared, was *not* dependent upon England ; His Majesty's subjects in Ireland were not, legally, to be deprived of their rights as free men. Meanwhile, he would exhort his countrymen, suffering as they did under all sorts of restrictive laws, to use every means within their power to better their condition.

His *Proposal For the Universal Use of Irish Manufacture* came out just before King George's sixtieth birthday. 'I hope, and believe,' Swift wrote, that 'nothing could please his Majesty better than to hear that his loyal Subjects, of both Sexes, in this Kingdom, celebrated his *Birth-Day* (now approaching) *universally* clad in their own Manufacture.' Let the Irish House of Commons make a Resolution against wearing any cloth in their families not of native wool and manufacture. Let them extend such a Resolution so as to stop all imports of silk, velvets, calicoes, 'and the whole

[1] See Louis A. Landa, 'Swift's Economic Views and Mercantilism', *Journal of English Literary History*, X (1943), 310-35.

Lexicon of Female Fopperies'. Let burying in wool be made compulsory by law, as in England. To crown all the rest, 'let a firm Resolution be taken, by *Male* and *Female*, never to appear with one single *Shred* that comes from *England; and let all the People say, AMEN.*'

Swift had here gone on to question England's right to bind men without their own consent. Reason, the Law of Nature, and the general opinion of men all agreed that under a limited form of government this right did not exist. It was because of such statements that the pamphlet was declared seditious and the printer, Edward Waters, prosecuted. The jury found Waters not guilty, but Lord Chief Justice Whitshed refused to accept the verdict, and the matter dragged on for another year, ending finally in a *noli prosequi*. Swift, again anticipating the Drapier, resorted to verse in order to bring this incident home to all patriotic Irishmen. *An Excellent new Song on a seditious Pamphlet. To the Tune of Packington's Pound* was, thanks to the broadest of irony, safe from prosecution, and one could roar out the refrain secure in the knowledge that Justice Whitshed could take no action :

> We'll buy *English* Silks for our Wives and
> our Daughters,
> In Spight of his Deanship and Journeyman
> *Waters.*

Once he had broken silence Swift proceeded to express himself on all sorts of current subjects. The bursting of the South Sea Bubble in August 1720, which added to Ireland's difficulties, brought from him at least one set of verses (*The Bubble* ; perhaps, too, *The Run upon the Bankers*). His enthusiastic approval of Archbishop King's Irish patriotism resulted in friendlier relations between the two men, which were reflected in the poem addressed to King (*Part of the 9th Ode of the 4th Book of Horace*). In January 1721 Swift wrote a notable letter to Pope—which the latter never received—in which he took occasion to review his life since leaving England, to tell the story of the prosecution in connexion with the *Proposal for the Universal Use of Irish Manufacture*, and to set forth his long-standing political principles in order, as he put it, to protect himself against the virulence of those libellers who had been busy fathering dangerous principles in government upon him. A proposal made about this time to establish a National Bank in Ireland stirred him to great activity, for along with many others in Dublin he saw dangers in the scheme that probably were not there. He seems to have been associated with many of the short publications ridiculing the Bank which were being circulated in Dublin at this time. He composed an *Epilogue* for a benefit performance of *Hamlet* given in April 1721 for the weavers in Dublin, who were then suffering from wide-spread unemployment. One of his minor impersonations is to be found in the *Last Speech and Dying Words of Ebenezor Elliston* (1722), which he arranged to be issued at the time of the execution of a notorious criminal—a composition entirely serious in purpose, in which Elliston is made to describe his life of crime as a warning to all his readers. *Some Arguments against Enlarging the Powers of Bishops In letting of Leases* is dated 21 October 1723 and had as its occasion a proposal to alter by law the terms under which the Irish Bishops could set their lands out to lease. The bill which then lay before the Irish House of Commons was in reality a device on the part of the landed gentry to reduce the possessions of the Church, and as such it was widely resented both by the bishops and the clergy as a whole.[1] None of these episodes and none of the writings—the *Proposal for the Universal Use of Irish Manufactures* excepted—is in itself of any exceptional interest, but only the detailed record can give us a right sense of the great range of Swift's

---

[1] See Louis A. Landa, *Swift and the Church of Ireland*, pp. 97 f.

interests and the tremendous energy with which he entered into the *rôle* of Irish patriot and statesman.

Until old age and broken health brought his active career to a close in the later 1730s, Swift never ceased to exert himself in behalf of the country and the public welfare. He made speeches ; he wrote serious pamphlets, occasionally ironic ones. Those who transgressed his principles of patriotism he lashed unmercifully in verse satires, ballads, lampoons. He fought, in his own way, for what he believed to be the best interests of the Church. He gave generously to Dublin's charitable institutions and was on numerous committees and boards. But by far the most dramatic of all the incidents which marked his career as Irish patriot was that which found him, in the character of one M.B., represented as a Dublin linen drapier with a shop in St. Francis Street, assuming a foremost part in the war against Wood's copper money.

The story of Wood's halfpence, the wide-spread concern which they caused throughout Ireland, the appearance of the five successive *Drapier's Letters* in 1724, and the withdrawal of this monetary scheme by Walpole's Government the following year is a well-known one, and thanks to modern scholarship most of the details and all the important points have now been clearly established. Ireland may or may not have needed a larger supply of copper coins at this time, but the patent granted in 1722 to William Wood authorized him to issue an amount at least five times greater than any possible requirement. Furthermore, the terms of the patent provided no adequate safeguards against counterfeiting, and it was foreseen that the circulation of debased coins would have a tendency to drive gold and silver currency out of the country. The Irish had been consulted at no point. The grant had been made in England, the enormous profit which Wood was reported to be making was to be entirely at the expense of the Irish, and no thought seemed to have been given either to the country's present monetary needs

or to her previous disastrous experiences with debased currency. There was good reason for the cry of alarm which
went up from responsible groups in Dublin. In August
1722, shortly after the provisions of the patent had been
disclosed, the Commissioners of Revenue in Dublin protested, and in the following month they addressed a letter
directly to the Treasury in London. A year passed, and
Wood was preparing to ship his coins into the kingdom.
When the Irish Parliament met in September 1723 both
houses expressed their apprehension in Addresses to the
King. There was still no sign, however, that anyone in
England was aware of the steadily rising tide of resentment or had taken notice of any of the protests which had
been sent over, and not until March 1724 did news reach
Ireland that an official inquiry had been ordered in London.
But by that time Swift had gone into action and in the first
of the *Drapier's Letters* had called upon his compatriots to
boycott the halfpence. *A Letter To the Tradesmen, Shop-
Keepers, Farmers, and Country-People in General, of the Kingdom of Ireland* was written in February—when only extreme
measures seemed likely to change the situation—and published early in March. Two thousand copies of the pamphlets are said to have found their way into the hands of the
public in the course of a few weeks. Was Swift playing
a lone hand, or was he one of a circle planning and directing the campaign against the patent? It is impossible to
say, though it seems likely that the distribution of the
Drapier's Letters was owing, in part at least, to something
like organized effort.

During the summer the Committee of the English Privy
Council appointed to study the terms of the patent made
its report, on the strength of which the Council attempted
to pacify the Irish through a compromise, and ordered a
sharp reduction in the amount of the new coinage. This
satisfied no one in Ireland, Swift least of all. The second
of the *Letters, To Mr. Harding the Printer*, appeared on

5 August shortly after the first news of the Committee's report had reached Dublin. It attacked the new proposals, represented Wood—'this little impudent Hard-ware-Man' —as turning into ridicule 'the Direful Apprehensions of a whole Kingdom', and urged that the boycott be rigorously observed:

. . . Mr. *Wood* cannot touch a Hair of your Heads. You have all the Laws of God and Man on your Side. When he, or his Accomplices, offer you his Dross, it is but saying *No*, and you are safe. If a mad Man should come to my Shop with a Handful of Dirt raked out of the Kennel, and offer it in Payment for Ten Yards of Stuff, I would pity or laugh at him; or, if his Behaviour deserved it, kick him out of my Doors. And, if Mr. *Wood* comes to demand any Gold or Silver, or Commodities for which I have paid my Gold and Silver, in Exchange for Trash, can he deserve or expect better Treatment?

The third *Letter* appeared before the end of August—it was dated 25 August—and was likewise occasioned by the Report to the Privy Council, now available in printed form. Here the Drapier turned to a smaller audience of educated and influential men, addressing *Some Observations* to 'the Nobility and Gentry of the Kingdom of Ireland'. It is the constitutional aspect which is brought under discussion:

Were not the People of *Ireland* born as *free* as those of England? How have they forfeited their Freedom? Is not their *Parliament* as fair a *Representative* of the *People*, as that of *England*? And hath not their Privy Council as great, or a greater Share in the Administration of publick Affairs? Are they not Subjects of the same King? Does not the same *Sun* shine over them? And have they not the same *God* for their Protector? Am I a *Free-man* in *England*, and do I become a *Slave* in six Hours, by crossing the Channel?

In speaking of the recent action of the Privy Council, the Drapier uses the bluntest language; and then, calling into play a kind of grim irony, allows Wood to assume the sins of Walpole and his fellow ministers: 'The Matter is come to an Issue. His Majesty, *Pursuant to the Law*, hath left the *Field* open between *Wood* and the Kingdom of *Ireland*. *Wood* hath Liberty to *Offer* his Coin, and we have *Law*, *Reason*, *Liberty*, and *Necessity* to *Refuse* it . . .' Towards the end of the *Letter* occurs the striking passage in which the Drapier, explaining why one like himself has felt obligated to write on matters calling for a much better pen than his, likens Wood to the giant Goliath—'all over BRASS'—and himself to David, forced to attack with sling and stone.

The excitement in Dublin was now intense. From the presses came a steady stream of petitions and declarations, pamphlets, poems, and ballads, among the latter Swift's *Serious Poem Upon William Wood, Brasier, Tinker, Hard-Ware-Man, Coiner, Counterfeiter, Founder and Esquire* (September 1724). An effigy of Wood was hanged and then burnt after great ceremony, and the *Full and True Account of the solemn Procession to the Gallows, at the Execution of William Wood*, which appeared on that occasion, is attributed to the Dean. Grafton, the Lord Lieutenant, had been recalled, and the arrival of his successor, Lord Carteret, was being awaited with some apprehension. Ireland, it was said, was now being charged with disputing the royal prerogative, and Carteret was coming over to take a stronger line. The critical moment was obviously approaching, for if the new Lord Lieutenant could seize the initiative by playing skilfully upon popular fear and rumour, he might break up the boycott and the entire campaign would be over quickly. The Drapier's famous fourth *Letter*, *To the Whole People of Ireland*, was designed to rally the patriots to renewed resistance. Its publication was timed to coincide with Carteret's arrival in Dublin on 22 October. The constitutional question had been raised in the previous *Letter*, but there the Drapier had been addressing a select audience. In the *Letter to the Whole People of Ireland* he is going over the same ground, but doing so in a strikingly different manner. Here he is the public orator, impressive in bearing, dramatic in statement. It is said that by refusing to receive Wood's money 'we *dispute the King's Prerogative; are grown ripe for Rebellion, and ready to shake off the Dependency of* Ireland *upon the Crown of* England.' But is it not the English in Ireland who have reduced the Kingdom to the obedience of England? And for this 'we have been rewarded with a worse Climate, the Privelege of being governed by Laws to which we do not consent; a ruined Trade, a House of *Peers* without *Jurisdiction*; almost an Incapacity for all Employments, and the Dread of *Wood's* Half-pence.' Then come, at length, the resounding words in which Ireland's dependency is explicitly denied and the nation is called upon to assert its political equality:

. . . I declare, next under God, I *depend* only on the King my Sovereign, and on the Laws of my own Country, And I am so far from *depending* upon the People of *England*, that, if they should ever *rebel* against my Sovereign, (which GOD forbid) I would be ready at the first Command from his Majesty to take Arms against them . . .

As for Wood's halfpence and the report of the Committee, the remedy

is wholly in your own Hands; and therefore I have digressed a little, in order to refresh and continue that *Spirit* so seasonably raised amongst you; and to let you see, that by the Laws of GOD, of NATURE, of NATIONS, and of your own Country, you ARE and OUGHT to be as FREE a People as your Brethren in *England*.

It was fitting, too, that Carteret's arrival should be celebrated in verse. *An Epigram On Woods's Brass-Money* appropriately enlarged on the theme of brass:

> *CART'RET* was welcom'd to the Shore
> First with brazen Cannons Roar.
> To meet him next, the Soldier comes,
> With brazen Trumps and brazen Drums.

Approaching near the Town, he hears
The brazen Bells salute his Ears:
But when *Wood's* Brass begun to sound,
Guns, Trumpets, Drums, and Bells were
drown'd.

There promptly ensued, in direct consequence of the publication of the *Letter to the Whole People of Ireland*, the episode which brought the Drapier's career to its dramatic climax. Carteret and Swift were old acquaintances, who respected and understood one another. The Lord Lieutenant could not, however, overlook the challenge which had now been given by the Drapier, for official purposes still a writer of unknown identity. A Proclamation was issued against those 'seditious' passages of the fourth *Letter* in which Ireland's independency was asserted, and on 7 November Harding, the printer, was taken in custody. This was the sort of combat that Swift loved. Just a week after Harding's arrest there appeared, in the form of a broadside, the *Seasonable Advice to the Grand-Jury*. Harding's case did not come up, for it was the *Seasonable Advice* that the Jury was asked to find against, and refusing to do so, was dismissed. A new Grand Jury was promptly returned, and on the last day of the term, 28 November, showed itself even more recalcitrant than the previous one, for not only did it refuse to find against any of the Drapier's writings but went on instead to submit the Presentment—prepared by Swift and promptly published as *The Presentment of the Grand-Jury of the County of the City of Dublin*—in which it named 'all such Persons as have attempted, or shall endeavour by Fraud, or otherwise, to impose the said Halfpence upon us'. Not only had the Drapier scored a great personal triumph, but, as events were to prove, the battle against Wood had been virtually won. In the meantime Swift had been making more verses—*Prometheus* and two poems addressed to Archbishop King, who had refused to sign the Lord Lieutenant's Proclamation—and after the

Jury's final act of defiance he poured vitriol upon his old enemy Justice Whitshed, who had presided at Harding's trial, lampooning him in *Whitshed's Motto* and *Verses on the upright Judge*. The last of the *Drapier's Letters* to be published at this time came out on the closing day of the year. *To the Right Honourable the Lord Viscount Molesworth*, addressed to a prominent Whig, is quiet and confident in tone. It reviews the Drapier's previous writings and the Proclamation against them, restates his position against the dependency of Ireland, and serves as a reminder that the political principles by which he has been guided are those of the Whigs themselves, as proved in Molesworth's own works.

Wood surrendered his patent the following August, and on the 26th the news was proclaimed throughout Ireland. The Drapier had written two other letters, but these were for various reasons withheld at the time. The earlier, the *Letter to the Lord Chancellor Middleton*, is dated 26 October 1724. Signed not by the Drapier but by Swift himself, it was to have been the Dean's open acknowledgement, at the time of the Proclamation, of his authorship of all the pamphlets, but he was apparently advised not to make this final challenge. The seventh and last *Letter* is the *Humble Address To Both Houses of Parliament*, which was composed during the summer of 1725 but withheld from publication after news had come of the surrender of the patent. Swift was here bringing to the attention of the Irish Parliament a number of things which could be done for the benefit of the kingdom without encountering opposition from England. Concerted action had become possible, he felt, since the country was united as never before, 'all the *Regular Seeds* of *Party* and *Faction*' being entirely rooted out. The Drapier had indeed accomplished wonders. He had succeeded as had no one before him in bringing the people of Ireland together in a common cause, and something of the feeling of unity which had been experienced during the war against the halfpence was to be sustained for the rest of the century. The vision which he briefly allowed himself of a happy kingdom where all divisive forces had yielded once and for all to reason turned out, of course, to be illusion, but it tells us something—does it not?—of the temper of the man who was then putting the finishing touches to *Gulliver's Travels*.

The *Drapier's Letters* are a superb example of literary—perhaps we should say rhetorical—skill brought into play in the interests of a public cause. All that Swift had learned as a satirist, as a writer on every-day matters of politics and Church, and as a journalist and propagandist was sooner or later drawn upon in the course of his great pamphlet campaign of 1724-5. Reading the *Letters* today we are perhaps so fascinated by the imperious bearing of the Patriot Dean and his mastery of the occasion that we remain indifferent to the precise techniques which have been employed. Yet we recognize very considerable differences in tone from one *Letter* to another, and are aware that the manner of statement has been adjusted to the audience of the moment. It is the common people, the whole people of Ireland, who are being appealed to in *Letters* like the first and fourth; the quieter tone of the third *Letter* and of the two that were withheld was appropriate for men of position. Similarly, we see that the character of M.B., the Drapier, is another one of Swift's imaginative creations, though in this case the disguise is worn carelessly and is sometimes virtually discarded. One passage which repays close attention occurs in the first *Letter*. At the place in question the Drapier is indulging in the kind of exultant arithmetical calculation that the Examiner had once employed in order to expose Marlborough. He begins with a reasonable enough statement: the weight of Wood's halfpence is between four and five to the ounce. Then, without warning, he takes us into a fantastic world which is suffering from a plethora of halfpence. The ounce, indeed!

Here they reckon them by the horse-load. A well-to-do farmer coming up to town to pay his half-year's rent must use a three-horse team; a squire on a shopping expedition has to bring five or six horses laden with sacks of the half-pence; it takes two hundred and fifty horses to transport rich Squire Conolly's half-year rents, and sometimes a team of twelve hundred to settle the accounts of the bankers. Satiric imagination, it is true, was presiding over this comedy of exaggeration, but the unique situation being portrayed had in a sense not been created by the Drapier at all. It was merely being taken over from an altogether real and contemporary world. That is the final comedy. If Wood had had his way, twelve-hundred-horse teams would not, perhaps, have been common sights in the streets of Dublin, but Ireland would have been overflowing with his halfpence.

Swift's energy and creative powers were perhaps never at a higher point than during these years which saw him emerge from seclusion to assume the patriot's *rôle* and, during the excitement over the halfpence, the character of the Drapier of St. Francis Street. His pamphlets and verses on public affairs, enough to keep most men fully occupied, were but a part of the achievement of this notable period. *Gulliver's Travels*, be it remembered, was taking shape. Also belonging to this time are several poems and short prose works, all non-controversial in character, which are to be recognized as exceptional for one reason or another.

The earliest of such prose pieces is the *Letter to a Young Gentleman, Lately enter'd into Holy Orders*, which first appeared in Dublin in 1720. There could have been no secret about Swift's authorship, and the London edition which came out shortly afterwards bore on the title-page a notice which informed the reader that the treatise had, as was certainly known, been written 'in Ireland by the Reverend Dr. Swift'. However, in the *Letter* itself the writer is represented as a 'Person of Quality', and the point of view from which he is offering his advice is consistently that of a cultivated layman. Swift's topic was the art of the sermon, and he was only saying the things he would have said—and often did—in his own person, but by speaking through the character of a man of quality he could suggest the right social values without further ado. There had been countless discourses before this on pulpit oratory, on the rhetoric of preaching, and on the subject-matter and approach proper to the sermon, and since the Restoration these had played a very important part in establishing among the Anglican clergy the stylistic principles of an age which had come to reject the baroque in favour of a manner of thought and statement which by design was simple, clear, direct. But it was not often that those who had to listen to sermons were allowed to voice their opinion. Here, for once, the clergy were offered some non-professional counsel. The result is not only an amusing and entertaining essay, but one containing some of Swift's clearest statements on prose style generally. The young preacher is warned against both pedantry and any ill-considered reaction against it : obscure terms are to be avoided, but so is the quaint, terse, florid style which is sometimes thought to display a knowledge of the world. Style may be defined as proper words in proper places. When a man's thoughts are clear, 'the properest Words will generally offer themselves first ; and his own Judgment will direct him in what Order to place these, so as they may be best understood'. There follows a noteworthy passage on what the Person of Honour calls the 'moving manner of Preaching'. The entire discussion at this point assumes added importance when it is realized how conscious a rhetorician Swift was in all of his satires. The purpose of oratory is to achieve practical results, 'to drive some one particular Point', which it sometimes does by arguments offered to the understanding and reason, sometimes by appealing to the emotions. It is rhetoric of the latter sort which the preacher is urged to avoid, on the grounds that he can best direct Christian men in the conduct of their lives through plain, convincing reasons. The talent of moving the passions is of small use in the pulpit:

I therefore entreat you to make use of this Faculty (if you be ever so unfortunate as to think you have it) as seldom, and with as much Caution as you can; else I may probably have Occasion to say of you, as a great Person said of another upon this very Subject. A Lady asked him, coming out of Church, whether it were not a very moving Discourse? *Yes,* said he, *I was extremely sorry, for the Man is my Friend.*

This is a paragraph which only Swift could have turned. What is expressed reflects, however, the quality of an age —perhaps not the eighteenth century proper, which had already been invaded by sensibility, but the earlier, severer period in which Swift had grown up.

The *Letter to a Young Lady, On Her Marriage* was written in February 1723, occasioned by the marriage the previous month of John Rochfort, son of Baron Rochfort—Swift was a frequent guest at the Baron's house at Gaulstown— to a girl by the name of Deborah Staunton. It is at once a traditional Letter of Advice, something in the manner of Halifax's famous *Advice to a Daughter*, and a personal greeting. It is of particular interest for several reasons. As the *Letter to a Young Gentleman* contains a warning against emotional preaching, so this is emphatic in its counsel against all romantic notions of marriage. The grand affair in the life of any married woman is to gain and preserve the friendship and esteem of her husband. 'I hope,' Swift goes on,

you do not still dream of Charms and Raptures; which Marriage ever did, and ever will put a sudden End to. Besides, yours was a Match of Prudence, and common Good-liking, without any Mixture of that ridiculous Passion which hath no Being, but in Play-Books and Romances.

The modern reader would be quite wrong in taking this as anti-feminism. As a matter of fact, Swift's view of woman as the equal of man in all intellectual respects is being affirmed throughout the *Letter*. There is no quality 'whereby Women endeavour to distinguish themselves from Men, for which they are not just so much the worse'. It is by improving her mind that the young lady may best win her husband's friendship, and the Dean undertakes to lay down for her 'a method of study' which she is advised—rather formidably, to be sure—to pursue closely. The good society as Swift conceived it may have been highly exclusive, but it was one in which men and women met on terms of complete equality. One further aspect of the *Letter* which is most enlightening concerns his advice relating to 'cleanliness and sweetness' of person. It is not Swift's feeling free to hold forth on such a subject but the manner in which he does so that is significant. The following passage has its parallels in certain of the poems and in *Gulliver's Travels*. Is it not also reminiscent of moments in Restoration comedy?

. . . the satyrical Part of Mankind will needs believe, that it is not impossible, to be very fine and very filthy; and that the Capacities of a Lady are sometimes apt to fall short in cultivating Cleanliness and Finery together. I shall only add, upon so tender a Subject, what a pleasant Gentleman said concerning a silly Woman of Quality; that nothing could make her supportable but cutting off her Head; for his Ears were offended by her Tongue, and his Nose by her Hair and Teeth.

A third *Letter*—this of *Advice to a Young Poet*—made its appearance in Dublin in 1721, and although signed with the initials E.F. has generally passed as Swift's work. There is now, however, considerable doubt as to his authorship. The irony is in the Dean's manner, and the narrowing of the term poetry to the productions of modern wits of questionable faith and morals seems to be an echo of the *Tale of a Tub*.

There are four or five poems which today stand out from

the others of this period. *To Mr. Delany* (1718) has for subject the true nature of raillery, and goes on to define that quality as well as the associated ones of wit and humour. What Swift said here on the subject of humour was to be amplified in the later essay on Gay and the *Beggar's Opera* (No. 3 of the *Intelligencer*, May 1728). The three Progress poems of 1719-20 are particularly striking. *Phillis, or, The Progress of Love* is a kind of moral fable, telling of the squalid life into which hero and heroine descend after their ill-advised elopement. *The Progress of Poetry* deals not with descent but flight—the flight of the goose, the flight of the half-starved Grub-Street poet as the vapours generated by hunger carry him aloft. *The Progress of Beauty* is one of Swift's minor masterpieces. The framework, as in the *Progress of Poetry*, is an analogy, in this case of the moon and the nymph, and the ruthlessness with which the parallelism is developed is enhanced by certain imitations of the Caroline manner, with parody becoming full-fledged in the closing stanza.

Along with these we should perhaps place the *Description of an Irish Feast*, Swift's translation of portions of an Irish poem. Here his energy is fully engaged by the rhythmic pattern—

> The Floor is all wet
>   With Leaps and with Jumps,
> While the Water and Sweat,
>   Splish, splash in their Pumps—

and in place of ruthlessly pursued analogies we have a delighted glimpse of Irish peasant life. But it was not often that Swift—or any of his contemporaries—consented to yield in this total way to the beat and sound of words.

VII

LEMUEL GULLIVER, WORLD TRAVELLER

GULLIVER'S TRAVELS appeared in print for the first time on 28 October 1726. Its immediate and tremendous success was not a matter of chance. Let us remember that it had been perfectly calculated for the taste of the age—an age which understood satiric comedy and was prepared for commentary on the human scene which was at once serious in its intent and witty and ingenious in its presentation. Swift had emphasized his 'moral' purpose when he had written to Pope that his chief end was 'to vex the world rather than divert it'. But neither he nor Pope ever imagined that what vexed could not also be infinitely diverting. When the *Travels* had first been offered to Benjamin Motte, the publisher, he had been assured that they would sell very well, despite the fact that they were perhaps a little satirical in one or two places. And Arbuthnot's remark, in a letter written to Swift after the success of the book was an assured fact, can be taken as expressing what a great many readers of 1726 undoubtedly felt: 'Gulliver is a happy man that at his age can write such a merry work.' A merry work! Could anything convey to us a clearer sense of the kind of audience Swift was writing for, or better persuade us of the skill with which he had addressed himself to it?

The first edition was soon exhausted, and before the end of the year two more were called for. But this was only the beginning. There were further editions in London, two different publishers brought the book out in Dublin, it was summarized and abridged, serialized in the newspapers, and in time translated into French, Dutch, and German. The appeal which it now holds for children has sometimes been pointed to as the final irony of Swift's career: the

satire intended to put mankind to shame ends up as popular
juvenile reading! But the truth is that *Gulliver's Travels*
has delighted the young from the day of its earliest appearance. This we have on the word of Gay and Pope, who
were careful to keep Swift posted during the period immediately following publication, and reported that it was universally read, 'from the cabinet-council to the nursery'. Its
course in the world, like that of every great book, has been
varied, and is in itself a fascinating and revealing subject.
It has been as fiercely repudiated as any classic in the English
language, it has been subject to incredible misinterpretation, yet there has never been a time when it did not rank
among the books most frequently read, and it has always
had defenders. It would be too much to say that there is
now general agreement about its meaning and its effect as
satiric statement. In matters of this sort one can only speak
of trends. Swift's moral realism—his insistence upon the
inside of things rather than the outside, upon actuality
rather than illusion, on the undisguised truth regarding
human nature and the human situation—is probably better
understood today than at any time since the earlier eighteenth century. It is not a question of full response, for that
we can never give—Swift's mind and sensibilities were controlled by an order of experience which in so many respects
must remain foreign to us. But what used to be called
Swift's pessimism strikes most of us today as merely common sense, and if *Gulliver's Travels* is placed beside some
of our own satiric writings—to say nothing of modern
existentialist plays and novels—it may, indeed, seem a comparatively cheerful book. However that may be, one can
at least say that its positive doctrines no longer repel instantly
and violently. Furthermore we are now probably readier
to perceive the artistry and craftsmanship which have gone
into the work, readier to acknowledge that its meaning as
an imaginative statement is not to be completely identified with any merely logical or common-sense meanings

which it may carry. *Gulliver's Travels* may be admirable commentary, but that is scarcely the reason of its long-continued appeal. It is Swift's comic artistry—the vision and the idiom—which has kept it alive.

The early history of *Gulliver's Travels* may be taken to include Swift's materials, his intentions as a writer, the manner in which the satire took shape, and the circum-stances attending its appearance as a printed book. If we are at all concerned with such matters, it is important that we distinguish between what is clearly established fact and what is, and in many cases must remain, conjecture. We know that Swift was a great reader of books of travel, long a favourite form of letters in England and on the continent ; he must have had more than a passing acquaintance with the *voyages imaginaires* turned out by seventeenth-century and contemporary French writers ; and like any educated man of his time he was familiar with, at the least, the fan-tastic voyages of Lucian and the Utopian accounts of Plato and More. The basic pattern of *Gulliver's Travels*—the vehicle of the traveller's account together with satiric com-mentary arising from the portrayal of fanciful communities —is perhaps its least original feature. It is impossible to say when Swift first sensed the possibilities afforded by a satiric narrative of this kind. The *Spectator* for 27 April 1711 (No. 50) told of four Indian kings lately in England and went on to give a summary of the journal said to have been kept by one of them during his visit. The next day Swift took note of this in the *Journal to Stella* :

The *Spectator* is written by Steele, with Addison's help; 'tis often very pretty. Yesterday it was made of a noble hint I gave him long ago for his *Tatlers*, about an Indian supposed to write his travels into England. I repent he ever had it. I intended to have written a book on that subject.

And, as we have previously seen, the supposed narrator in the *New Journey to Paris* (Sept. 1711), the Sieur du Baudrier, comes at one point to bear a striking resemblance to Lemuel Gulliver. But it has been generally supposed that Swift's first actual experiments in satiric narration of this type were undertaken as a member of the Scriblerus Club. This famous literary group, strongly Tory in character and serving as a kind of counterbalance to the Whig circle which had grown up about Addison and Steele, was organized in the autumn of 1713, having as active members Swift, Arbuthnot, Parnell, Pope, and Gay. It was proposed that the Club undertake some sort of joint satiric composition, and finally it was settled that this should take the form of a mock biography of a universal pedant—'a man', as Pope was later to describe him, 'of capacity enough; that had dipped into every art and science, but injudiciously in each'. Years were to pass before the *Memoirs of Martinus Scriblerus* was to appear in print—Pope published it in 1741 in the second volume of his *Prose Works*—but much of it must have been written during the period of the Club's greatest activity, which fell between February and June 1714. Swift's part in this joint enterprise cannot be positively established. The sixteenth chapter of the *Memoirs* as published in 1741 gives an account of Scriblerus's travels, four in number and similar in character to Gulliver's; and Pope told Spence that it was from the *Memoirs* that Swift took his first hints for *Gulliver*. We have no assurance, however, that the chapter in question existed in 1714. It could have been added at any time prior to 1741, and it is perfectly possible that Pope worked it out and inserted it just before the publication of the *Memoirs*, since it had been a game of long standing with the Scriblerians to father all sorts of works upon their hero, and Swift would have been the last to protest this final attribution. But though this account of Scriblerus's travels may have been a good-natured hoax designed to increase the sales of the *Memoirs*, there is still every reason to believe that part of the original plan was to send Martin on various extraordinary voyages, and that these voyages were discussed by the Club members at their meetings in 1714. Did Swift, taking the matter up, begin an account of Martin's adventures? It seems entirely likely that this was the case. He must, however, have dropped the whole thing when he left London at the end of May 1714 for Letcombe Bassett, since by that time he had other work to occupy him and was in no mood for comedy. Nor, apparently, did he return to his travels during the long and discouraging period which began with his return to Dublin and extended down to about 1720. Thanks to the references to *Gulliver's Travels* which turn up in his correspondence—notably in the letters to his friend Charles Ford—we know that he was at work on his satire by 1721, that Parts I and II had been finished by the end of 1723 and Part IV by January 1724, and that in the latter year he was engaged on Part III. In August 1725 he announced that the work was finished and that he was then revising and transcribing it.

To what extent had he made use of Scriblerian materials? Opinion is divided. The generally accepted view is that portions of the first and third voyages go back to some version dating from 1714; and certain discrepancies of detail in Parts I and III seem to show where old and new portions have been joined. It has recently been argued, on the other hand, that when Swift began writing in 1721 there was no earlier draft in existence, the entire work as we have it being of one piece.[1] These theories about the composition of *Gulliver's Travels* involve the allusions to contemporary events and the nature of the political allegory. The political allegory will be taken up in due course and can be passed over at this point. The question immediately before us concerns, not details, but rather the total effect conveyed by the finished satire. Whether or not *Gulliver's Travels* embodies an older plan and older fragments, all

[1] I refer to Arthur Case's discussion of this matter in his *Four Essays on 'Gulliver's Travels'* (Princeton, N.J., 1945).

going back to the activities of the Scriblerus Club in 1714, is not, perhaps, a matter of great interest to most readers. Yet there are certainly a number of inconsistencies in the narrative, and though many of these would probably go unobserved by anyone who chose to dispense with notes and commentaries, there are some which force themselves upon our attention. For instance, the Utopian account of Lilliputian civilization (Part I, Chap. vi) comes to us as something of a surprise. The preceding episodes have displayed the little people as anything but admirable, and we may not be left entirely satisfied by Gulliver's explanation that in his account he 'would only be understood to mean the original Institutions, and not the most scandalous Corruptions into which these People are fallen by the degenerate Nature of Man.' This is one of several inconsistencies occurring in Parts I and III which support the view that when Swift settled down to work in 1721 he had before him an earlier draft, however fragmentary, and wove a certain amount of older material into the new texture. The contrary theory, according to which *Gulliver's Travels* is all new writing without any patchwork at all, attempts to establish for Parts I and III a consistency of allusion, political allegory, and specific intent that is not wholly convincing. But whichever way we may be led to interpret the evidence, we ought not to lose sight of the fact that Swift's plan and his tactical execution of it are to be judged by the achievement. What matters is not Swift's time-schedule but the satiric masterpiece which was constructed. However they got there, the inconsistencies of detail are part of the total effect. Whether they enhance this effect or not—an interesting question—they certainly do not seriously mar it.

In any case, Swift had a finished manuscript in hand by the autumn of 1725, and the time had come to think of a printer. During all the years which had passed since Queen Anne's death he had not once returned to England or wanted to, but time had now brought about a number of changes. The Tories had never recovered from the great reverse of 1714, but the high tide of their opponents' fury had passed and Bolingbroke had returned from exile. Swift had scored a famous victory over Walpole in the Wood affair. His old companions of the Scriblerus Club were impatient to learn more of his new satire and urging him to pay them a visit. And now the need of finding a publisher. Swift crossed in March 1726 and remained in England for five months, departing from London on 15 August. During this period he saw much of Pope, Gay, Arbuthnot, and Charles Ford, and visited Pope at Twickenham. It is not unlikely that his satire, still in manuscript, received the direct attention of his friends and particularly of Arbuthnot, for the Doctor had previously written to Swift urging him not to put the finishing touches to his work until better acquainted 'with some of the new improvements of mankind, that have appeared of late, and are daily appearing'. If Arbuthnot supplied new materials it was in all probability for the Laputan projects described in the third voyage, and some of the sources which seem to have been drawn upon for this part of *Gulliver's Travels* suggest that additions were in fact made in 1726. The problem of negotiating with a publisher was solved in a manner characteristic of the Scriblerus Club. That there should have been a problem was owing in part to Swift's fear of possible prosecution, in part to his instinct to play up to the fiction that Lemuel Gulliver was indeed the author of the *Travels*, and not a little to the Scriblerians' love of sport. Still another character was now devised, and Richard Sympson, cousin to Mr. Lemuel Gulliver, was set to work to draw up a letter to Motte. This letter, dated 8 August, offered the *Travels* for publication, stipulated terms, and was dropped at Motte's along with a sample of the work in manuscript. Motte accepted with alacrity, and in due course received the rest of the manuscript. Swift had then left London, but this concluding episode of the plot was reported to him by Pope.

'Motte,' he wrote, 'received the copy, he tells me, he knew not from whence, nor from whom, dropped at his house in the dark, from a hackney coach.' The original edition, in two octavo volumes, appeared on 28 October 1726.

London's response—immediate and mostly enthusiastic —was reported to Swift in some detail by his fellow Scriblerians, who were in high spirits over the book's success. On several occasions they commented on Part III. 'I tell you freely,' wrote Arbuthnot, 'the part of the projectors is the least brilliant.' And Gay and Pope had this to say :

As to other critics, they think the flying island is the least entertaining; and so great an opinion the town have of the impossibility of Gulliver's writing at all below himself, it is agreed that part was not writ by the same hand . . .

These remarks strongly suggest that the Club had contributed to Part III and was amused by the reactions to this portion of the satire.

When the book which Motte had published reached him in Ireland, Swift found that it contained many errors of the press, and he complained to Pope of several passages which appeared to be patched or altered. A list of minor corrections was made, and this Motte made use of in the octavo edition which he put out in 1727 (called on the title-page the second edition, but actually his fourth octavo edition). But the patched or altered passages referred to in the letter to Pope were to remain as in the original edition of 1726 until Faulkner, the Dublin printer, with Swift's co-operation, corrected them in his 1735 edition of the *Travels* (Vol. III of the collected *Works*). Even so, a long passage at the end of the third chapter of Part III was not to appear in print until 1896. The Faulkner edition—with the addition of the passage just referred to—would seem to represent the text of *Gulliver's Travels* which Swift wished us to have and into which he had introduced certain changes of wording going beyond the mere correction of the errors made by Motte.[1]

As has been suggested, the early history of *Gulliver's Travels* may be taken to include further matters than those already touched upon, for Swift's manner of work raises the question of what his materials chiefly consisted of. Since he was writing an imaginary voyage, he naturally looked to the extensive literature of travel, real and imaginary. He drew upon Rabelais and other satirists. As has recently been shown, the scientific projects described in Part III display an acquaintance with a wide variety of current projects and experiments and with the work of the members of the Royal Society as reported in the *Philosophical Transactions*, and the flying island owes something both to Gilbert's theories of magnetism and contemporary discussion arising in connexion with Halley's comet.[2] Finally there are recognizable elements of political allegory present in both the first and the third Parts, the allusions being to people and events in the England of Anne and George I. Certain of the references are unmistakable, but there are others that are open to different interpretations. What we make of the latter and, indeed, of Swift's basic intentions as a political allegorist will depend upon our notion of how the *Travels* was put together. There is agreement that the latter part of Gulliver's experiences in Lilliput—the ingratitude he meets with after performing the signal feat of capturing the enemy's entire fleet, the sentence passed on him, and his flight to the neighbouring kingdom of Blefuscu—is a thinly-veiled allegory of Bolingbroke's fate subsequent to the Queen's death. It is also clear that Bolgolam points to

[1] For a full discussion of all these matters, see Sir Harold Williams, *The Text of 'Gulliver's Travels'* (Cambridge, 1952).

[2] See the two illuminating articles by Marjorie Nicolson and Nora M. Mohler: 'The Scientific Background of Swift's *Voyage to Laputa*', *Annals of Science*, II (1937), 299-334; and 'Swift's "Flying Island" in the *Voyage to Laputa*', *Annals of Science*, II (1937), 405-430.

the Earl of Nottingham and Flimnap to Walpole, and a recent interpretation[1] which is convincing identifies Reldresal with Charles, Viscount Townshend, who succeeded Bolingbroke as Secretary of State. The theory that Part I embodies material dating from 1714 and that this material was worked into the newer portions rests in part upon what have been taken to be inconsistencies seeming to denote a shift in intent and focus. In the earlier episodes in this voyage—so the reasoning goes—Gulliver bears no resemblance to Bolingbroke, the Emperor does not suggest any English sovereign, and Lilliput is merely itself, a wholly imaginary community; but when Swift took up the story after a lapse of some seven years he introduced an allegorical theme not originally present, and in consequence the Emperor was given a resemblance to George I, Gulliver to Bolingbroke, and Flimnap—originally a colourless character —to Walpole.[2] But it has been argued, as we have seen, that the voyage to Lilliput was written entirely after 1721, and on this theory there has been constructed a somewhat different reading according to which all of Gulliver's adventures during the first voyage are part of a hidden history of the Oxford-Bolingbroke Ministry:[3] the shipwreck in Chapter i takes us back to the reverse suffered by Harley and St. John in 1708, two years before they came to power; Bolgolam's animosity to Gulliver is Nottingham's opposition to the Tory Ministry late in 1711; the fire in the Queen's palace is the War of the Spanish Succession, and Gulliver's quenching of it is the peace negotiated by Bolingbroke and Oxford; the articles of impeachment drawn up against Gulliver are the charges made against Oxford and Bolingbroke after Anne's death. Some of these latter

[1] cf. Case, op. cit., p. 78.

[2] The interpretations here referred to are those of Sir Charles Firth as set forth in 1919 in his well-known essay on 'The Political Significance of "Gulliver's Travels"', now reprinted in his *Essays Historical and Literary* (Oxford, 1938).   [3] Case, op. cit.

interpretations may, however, be accepted, particularly that of the articles of impeachment, without giving up the view that Part I was written at different times and lacks perfect consistency. The allegory in Part III raises the same kind of questions. Is it consistent, revealing a single plan, or does it give evidence of both earlier and later writing? The voyage as a whole seems to lack the unity of the others, and this impression remains despite the recent attempt to persuade us that it was all written in the 1720s and carefully designed to carry the allegory of Part I forward into the reign of George I and so to shadow forth the lamentable state of affairs brought to pass by the Whigs.[1] The flying island does undoubtedly signify, if not England, at least the power of the state and the tyrannical exercise of such power; and the story of the rebellion in Lindalino—or Dublin—and the manner in which it defended itself against the King and the island hovering overhead leaves no doubt in any reader's mind that the Wood affair and Ireland's successful resistance of the patent are intended. The character of Munodi was probably created with Oxford in mind, and the abandoned mill on his estate is very likely a symbol of the South Sea enterprise, established under Oxford but going down to ruin under the Whigs in 1720. In sum, we may say that much has come to light concerning the political allegory which Swift introduced into the first and third Parts—enough, at least, to assure us that his intentions in this respect were more than casual. But it would be a mistake to see either of these Parts as dominated by such intentions. *Gulliver's Travels* is a satiric comedy cast in the form of the imaginary voyage. The allegorical elements, whatever they are and however they came there, have not been allowed to encroach on the comedy or break up the form.

Today we are fully aware that the total meaning of a literary work, be it poem, play, or novel, derives only in

[1] Case, op. cit.

part from the theories, intellectual and moral, which are present in it. In considering the literary art of the Enlightenment we must, however, bear in mind the way in which the critical-aesthetic principles of the age—the principles deriving from the theory of imitation—affected the presentation of ideas and doctrines appearing in the imaginative work. Literature 'pleased'—an abrupt way of acknowledging both the techniques of expression and the aesthetic qualities differentiating art from matter-of-fact statement. But it also and very definitely had the function of instructing: it was addressed to normal men, it enforced normality of experience and conduct, it conveyed ideas, it afforded both moral and intellectual commentary. It cannot be said too often that *Gulliver's Travels* is in the end to be understood only as an artistic statement. At the same time it is proper to insist that it is eighteenth-century commentary in the precise sense. It has a solid core of intellectual meaning, it presents certain specific theories and principles about man and society. When we are told by one modern commentator that it is to be recognized 'as the final and completest satire on human life of [a] Christian moralist', and by another that it has behind it 'a world-view which only just passes the test of sanity', something would seem to be the matter with our triangulation. What follows immediately is an attempt to answer the straightforward question, 'What does *Gulliver's Travels* "say"?', in an entirely straightforward manner.

Society, we are told for one thing, lies in perpetual danger of corruption. Such time prospects as we are given in the course of the book are all historical, extending from the present backwards into the past and revealing the law of degeneration to which men and human circumstances are forever subject. The original institutions of Lilliput were admirable, but later the people fell into 'the most scandalous Corruptions' by the 'degenerate Nature of Man'. The king of Brobdingnag, informed by Gulliver of European manners and customs, detects therein 'some Lines of an Institution, which in its Original might have been tolerable'. The Vision of the Dead in the third Voyage (Chaps. vii and viii) affords several contrasts between the past and present—the Roman senate and a modern parliament, English yeomen 'of the old Stamp' and their grandchildren—which illustrate the degenerative trend. The Houyhnhnms have a general tradition that the Yahoos are not native to the country but descendants of two brutes once seen together upon a mountain, and Gulliver's master—with hints from Gulliver—advances the theory that these two progenitors, driven thither over the sea and coming to land, were forsaken by their companions, retired to the mountains, 'and degenerating by Degrees, became in Process of Time, much more savage than those of their own Species in the Country from whence these two Originals came.' This theory of history and of human behaviour can perhaps be called pessimistic, but the degree and quality of the pessimism involved have been badly misjudged. There was as yet no widely accepted myth of progress, no vision of social perfection awaiting mankind in the future. The Christian view of fallen man, the moral view, still conditioned most minds, and found no essential contradiction in the theory of politics and history which Swift had taken over from his classical and modern sources. Morally, man faced the obligation of asserting reason over brute instinct; socially and politically, he was to learn from history the means of prolonging the life of the civilized state, which though limited by laws of nature might be preserved into old age by prudence. The pessimism inherent in such doctrines is not that of despair, but of a moral realism counselling resolution and modified hope.

On the score of social theory, *Gulliver's Travels* may be said to rest on doctrines which, however much they were at odds with the middle-class civilization which was establishing itself in England, still controlled the thought of most traditionalists, including a large part of the established clergy. Social stratification presented itself as inevitable and proper, and the principle of degree, by which everyone has his appointed place and is to acknowledge the obligations attaching to it, corresponded to the links in the chain of being, the gradations in the created universe. It was an older concept of the organized community. It was not democratic, but to pronounce it anti-democratic is to wrest it from its historical context and to attribute motives that in the case of Swift simply did not exist. As social theorist the worst that he can justifiably be called is clerical. The Lilliputian and Brobdingnagian societies both reveal established and recognized social scales. Among the Houyhnhnms there is an inferior class 'bred up to be Servants'. And in the Utopia sketched in the first voyage the education a person receives is suitable to his position in society: there are nurseries for children of noble and eminent birth, nurseries for children 'of ordinary Gentlemen, Merchants, Traders, and Handicrafts'; boys designed for trades leave school at the age of seven to be apprenticed; the children of cottagers and labourers are kept at home, their business 'being only to till and cultivate the Earth' and their education consequently 'of little Consequence to the Public'. But there is equality for women. In the female nurseries Gulliver is unable to perceive any substantial difference in the education given to young girls, and we may remember that the Houyhnhnms find the idea of one kind of education for men and another for women a monstrous one.

It remained for a later time to discern human conflict as class struggle. That there was conflict and that this was in the nature of things and according to certain discoverable laws Swift firmly believed. It was, however, a political rather than an economic-social set of equations which he had worked out in order to explain history and give us a certain measure of control over events. His theory of the three estates and of the balance of power, 'to be carefully held by every State within it self', served both as analysis of the realities disclosed in history and as his central doctrine of rational or constitutional freedom, for as he had written years before in the *Contests and Dissensions*, 'In all Free States the Evil to be avoided is *Tyranny*, that is to say, the *Summa Imperii*, or unlimited Power solely in the Hands of the *One*, or the *Few*, or the *Many*.' His recent championship of the cause of Irish independence had been a battle in behalf of such rational liberty. The emphasis placed by both the Lilliputians and the King of Brobdingnag on common sense as against *expertise* in government is an essential part of this theory of freedom, and the suspicion of standing armies in time of peace expressed by the King follows directly from it. The political intrigues into which the Lilliputians have fallen in their degenerate condition and, in contrast, the avoidance of all such absurdities in partyless Brobdingnag point, perhaps, to that ideal of statesmanship above party which he had been wont to voice in the days of the Oxford Ministry. More direct and forthright as an expression of his passionate belief in liberty is the passage in Part III in which Caesar and Brutus are called up from the dead:

I was struck with a profound Veneration at the Sight of *Brutus*; and could easily discover the most consummate Virtue, the greatest Intrepidity, and Firmness of Mind, the truest Love of his Country, and general Benevolence for Mankind in every Lineament of his Countenance. I observed with much Pleasure, that these two Persons were in good Intelligence with each other; and *Caesar* freely confessed to me, that the greatest Actions of his own Life were not equal by many Degrees to the Glory of taking it away.

And as other ghosts are summoned up, Gulliver feasts his eyes 'with beholding the Destroyers of Tyrants and Usurpers, and the Restorers of Liberty to oppressed and injured Nations'.

When it is considered that *Gulliver's Travels* is an imaginary voyage it becomes apparent that the absence of certain themes long associated with this literary type is in itself almost a 'positive'. Throughout the seventeenth century the *voyage imaginaire* had been used by French writers of the *libertin* tradition as a vehicle for their naturalistic theories and as a means of subjecting established civilization and the culture of Europe to rationalistic criticism. The traveller habitually discovered some happy society where men lived the simple, uncorrupted life, instructed entirely by natural instinct and the innate light of reason; and from the vantage point of such a primitivistic Utopia European man was seen, in all his repulsiveness, as the victim of civilization and traditionalism. Gulliver's experiences are not of this order, for the people among whom he is cast are in no sense children of nature. They are all living in highly organized societies and are governed by institutions which Gulliver goes to much pains to describe. If in the end he develops an overwhelming aversion to everything at home, it is not because Europe suffers the evil of civilization but because it is losing its civilization and falling into a state of degenerate corruption. There is perhaps no other imaginary voyage as free as is *Gulliver's Travels* of anything resembling anti-traditionalism. It contains no criticism of religion, no anti-clericalism, and very little of even the minor details of cultural primitivism.

In addition to the things that have been mentioned, which form the framework of ideas on which the book rests, we have of course the more general themes of moral satire: man's pettiness and greed, his pride, the infinite perversion of reason, the absurdities and evils of the various professions. There is an amusing summary of these themes in the *Letter from Capt. Gulliver*, which though dated 1727 was not added to the text until 1735. Gulliver professes surprise that during the six months that his book has been in the hands of the public it has produced not a single effect according to his intentions. 'I desired,' he writes his cousin, Richard Sympson,

you would let me know by a Letter, when Party and Faction were extinguished; Judges learned and upright; Pleaders honest and modest,

with some Tincture of common Sense; and *Smithfield* blazing with
Pyramids of Law-Books; the young Nobility's Education entirely
changed; the Physicians banished; the Female *Yahoos* abounding in
Virtue, Honour, Truth and good Sense: Courts and Levees of great
Ministers thoroughly weeded and swept; Wit, Merit and Learning
rewarded; all Disgracers of the Press in Prose and Verse, condemned
to eat nothing but their own Cotten, and quench their Thirst with
their own Ink. These, and a Thousand other Reformations, I firmly
counted upon . . . as indeed they were plainly deducible from the
Precepts delivered in my Book.

As satiric comedy *Gulliver's Travels* is many things and
embraces many levels of intention and execution. Most
accounts of imaginary societies sooner or later give themselves away by allowing their underlying logic to become
too apparent—when there are no further surprises in store
the effect becomes one of monotony. In this sense there is
nothing obvious about *Gulliver's Travels*. It keeps our
interest at every point because we are never able to anticipate what is going to happen, and when it does happen
we are not always sure what our response should be. The
contradictory details and incongruities in the narrative, if
we observe them, add to our perplexities. Despite all the
differences between the *Tale of a Tub* and the *Travels*, the
two satires are alike in creating tension by means of the
uncertainties and surprises to which the reader is exposed.
The *Travels* begins for all the world like a genuine account
by an actual ship's surgeon, and the reader of 1726 might
well have wondered, until he came to Gulliver's awakening
after coming to shore, whether this was not a book of sober
fact. Gulliver is perfectly in character—a Cambridge man,
scientifically minded, curious to observe the manners and
dispositions of foreign lands, and an apt linguist. The
world was full of just such professional sailors who felt that
in publishing accounts of their travels they were contribut-
ing to scientific knowledge. Gulliver's prose style is the
kind which had the approval of the Royal Society; it is

seemingly matter-of-fact, free of literary colouring, recording observed details with the fullness and precision of some scientific instrument. As an imaginary voyage *Gulliver's Travels* is consummate parody which preserves much of the spirit, the imaginative principle, of the real voyages. But if this is the main contrast that runs through the book, we are sometimes aware of another one or at least the opportunity for another one, for there are moments when we have to ask ourselves whether our imaginary voyage is not becoming a parody of itself—whether, for instance, the Utopian elements are not slyly humorous. Furthermore, as the political allegory comes and goes we are left with further questions and further points of reference to keep track of. The tone modulates from that of harsh indictment of crime and folly to good-natured fantasy. It was once assumed that Gulliver and his creator were to all intents and purposes the same person, but the full realization that Swift has created a fictional character has not put an end to our troubles. To say that Gulliver is Gulliver, not Swift, merely raises a new set of questions. Who is Gulliver? What is it that happens to him? How have he and his experiences been contrived by this satirist who has succeeded in writing a merry work that has never ceased to vex the world?

Our problem is how to talk about the structure of *Gulliver's Travels*, the configuration presented by the whole book, in a way that will order our impressions and reveal things that are actually in the work of art without implying that any such analysis can ever capture the full meaning. Perhaps we can best do this by considering, one by one, certain patterns that seem to run through the book. The most obvious of these patterns has already been touched upon. Three strands enter into this: the account of actual travels, the imaginary voyage, and parody of the latter. To change our figures, we have a basic theme, a variation on it, and sometimes a variation on the variation. The Utopian passages in both the first and fourth voyages are looking in

two ways at once. The Lilliputians have—or had once—
many admirable institutions, but these sometimes overreach
themselves in the way that Utopian institutions have had
a habit of doing ever since Plato. The nurseries for children
of noble and eminent birth are run on admirable principles,
and it is no doubt well that there are provisions which make
it impossible for these children to be spoiled by their doting
parents, but only a confirmed Utopia-maker or one diabolic-
ally familiar with such a creature could have devised the
following :

Their Parents are suffered to see them only twice a year; the Visit
is not to last above an Hour; they are allowed to kiss the Child at
Meeting and Parting; but a Professor, who always standeth by on
those Occasions, will not suffer them to whisper, or use any fondling
Expressions, or bring any Presents of Toys, Sweet-meats, and the like.

The Utopia of horses, filled with the sound of whinnying,
hoofbeats, and the champing of oats, is a rational community, true enough, but in outdoing all other Utopias in
point of consistency the satire directed at man's irrationality
suggests that it might extend itself to include his dreams of
the good society.

A second pattern is the one underlying the sequence of
the four voyages. Is it a weakness that Part III should
intervene between Gulliver's experiences in Brobdingnag
and his later ones in the country of the Houyhnhnms?
However *Gulliver's Travels* was planned in this respect,
what is perhaps a fault from a purely logical point of view
seems to justify itself artistically. In the opening voyage we
are not sure for some time, nor is Gulliver, about the true
nature of the Lilliputians and their civilization, and though
eventually Gulliver has good cause to conclude that these
little people are as contemptible morally as they are small
in stature, this discovery does not leave him inwardly moved.
Part II is more rigorous than this. Not only are the experiences less ambiguous but they bite more deeply into

Gulliver's sensibilities. Part IV really begins, psychologically, where the second leaves off, for the intensity of Gulliver's reactions produces in him a state of shock which causes him to lose his self-esteem as one of the human race. The intervention of the third voyage, scattered in its effects and only once—in the episode of the Struldbrugs—producing a marked psychic reaction on Gulliver's part, is almost a functional necessity. Like the scherzo in a traditional four-movement symphony, it comes between the second and fourth movements to break the tension and prepare the way for a stronger climax than could otherwise be achieved. This is only one of a number of details which it is easy enough to make out in this sequential pattern. The contrast given us in the first two voyages between little men and big men may be an obvious one, but into it has gone the cosmic imagination of an age which had produced Boyle, Locke, and Sir Isaac Newton—an age which thought of man as stationed on the isthmus of his middle state but permitted to catch glimpses through microscope and telescope of the created forms that filled the universe. But if the pigmy-giant sequence might have occurred to almost anyone, the final sequence which takes us from societies of human beings into a world of animals is worthy of Swift's comic wit. Rational animals were not new, nor was the idea that man in abdicating reason sinks lower than the beasts. Swift's originality lies in devising a series of experiences of which the last is a violent and preposterous variation of those which have preceded: Gulliver, having seen himself in relation to little men and then big ones, is finally and suddenly forced into comparison not with men at all but animals. This last situation is further complicated in that the comparison is not simple but complex, for there are two orders of animals, between which poor Gulliver stands dubiously. For Swift and his original readers what was essentially involved in Part IV was an outrageous paradox. Man and animal belonged to different levels of creation, they were forms forever separate, related to one another not through any natural principles of growth and continuity but as links in the chain of being. The resolution of the paradox is afforded by the obvious moral symbolism which is present throughout the fourth voyage: man may so live as to be worthy of his God-given status; on the other hand he may, by forfeiting his humanity, become repulsive, bestial.

The last pattern that will be discussed is perhaps not quite on all fours with those previously mentioned. By means of it control is exercised over the book as a whole and over many of the details, but its presence in the structure itself is not so immediately apparent and has often, indeed, escaped observations altogether. We might, at the start, think of it as the ironic mode in which much of *Gulliver's Travels* has been cast. The irony in this instance is of a species that came naturally to more than one eighteenth-century writer, Goldsmith being another who understood its use. The narrative and dramatic literature of the Enlightenment dealt freely with current ideas, but did so in its own way. Theories about men and society appear constantly in the plays and narratives of the period, and frequently assume major importance as a thematic element. These concepts and principles are often brought before us in a perfectly direct and straightforward manner, and are to be understood as generalizations to which everyone—author and public alike—subscribes as a matter of course. But another method of presentation, often alternating with the first in the same work, is also employed. In the latter case the ideas are introduced through the distorting medium of some character who is made to voice them in his own fashion or to colour them with his own experience. The question where direct and public statement ends and dramatic presentation takes over is sometimes a nice one for the reader. What is straightforward, what—by virtue of a double point of view brought into play—is ironic? It is through the use he has made of his central character, Lemuel Gulliver, that Swift has created a masterpiece of eighteenth-century comic art. The positive doctrines and precepts appearing in the *Travels* were all of them familiar to his age. It is the ironic refraction supplied by Gulliver that produces the extra-ordinary effects.

Comedy, in Swift, is sometimes the comedy of discontinuity. We strip, we analyse, and are shocked by the discrepancy we find between appearance and reality. Again, we have what we come to recognize as comedy in terms of a special situation : a certain state of affairs begins to define itself, becomes increasingly and arrogantly certain of its own identity, and grows, expands, improvises, aggrandizes itself at the expense of everything within reach. The digressions of the *Tale* and the enthusiasm of Peter and Jack as depicted in the fable of the coats illustrate this latter mode. But the comedy of *Gulliver's Travels* is something different from these types—a comedy, we may call it, of exploration and exclusion. Only once in the course of all the four voyages do we have an episode which turns upon sudden exposure. When Gulliver, on hearing of the Struldbrugs, assumes that they are universally envied for their immortality he is permitted by his hosts to indulge in a rhapsody on the blessings of long life before being shown the repulsive truth. Ordinarily Gulliver is not deceived in this manner by outward appearances only to learn the actual state of affairs in a moment of horrible revelation. Nor has he created any of the situations in which he finds himself. He is projected by the forces of nature into a number of strange societies which he proceeds to explore somewhat in the manner of a modern cultural anthropologist. He is a perfectly normal Englishman, well-adjusted as we say today, who has never known what it means to be a misfit, an unacceptable eccentric, a pariah. When he awakens to find himself among the Lilliputians his first feeling is one of mingled astonishment and curiosity. The earlier experiences which he undergoes leave him of two minds about this society, for he sees the shortcomings of the little people and at the same time acquires genuine respect for their original institutions. But on further acquaintance the Lilliputians reveal themselves as thoroughly contemptible. They have, meanwhile, turned upon the giant in their midst, but by this time Gulliver's self-esteem is not to be affected by any judgement which such people can pass against him. He has made his explorations, he finds himself an object of hatred, but he in turn has rejected this entire society. Back again in England, he is psychologically quite unaltered. Brobdingnag produces a different sort of reaction. Again there is exploration, and again an element of uncertainty in the earlier stage. The first of the giants whom Gulliver encounters are not, save for Glumdalclitch, the 'little nurse', a particularly admirable people, and his first master almost works him to death out of sheer greed. Are the Brobdingnagians to prove as coarse in sentiment as they are big in size? When Gulliver reaches the court he finds that the aristocracy bear an entirely different character. Yet throughout his entire residence among the giants the sense of security which he has in the presence of this amiable race is mixed with a feeling of nausea caused by the sights and smells which he must endure. There is, however, nothing ambiguous about the judgement which is eventually passed, not upon Gulliver as an individual but upon Europeans as a people, who are declared to be 'the most pernicious Race of little odious Vermin that Nature ever suffered to crawl upon the Surface of the Earth'. This is a new experience for Gulliver, who for the first time in his life finds himself, always hitherto a normal and acceptable person, rejected as an unwholesome deviate. His response is to seek protection in a newly-acquired pride and to convince himself not only that the estimable characteristics of the Brobdingnagians are absurd but that European civilization has virtues which it clearly does not possess.

If the pattern we are speaking of—ironic refraction and the comedy of exclusion—almost drops from sight in Part III, it is the compositional principle behind the climactic fourth voyage. Here the exploratory element has been reduced to a minimum. From the first, by a flash of intuition—a mode of certainty Swift's age liked to talk about —Gulliver is convinced of the moral virtues of the Houyhnhnms, and the recognition scene in the second chapter—what a recognition scene it is!—leaves him under the necessity of acknowledging the close physical resemblance between himself and the detestable Yahoos. Part IV is almost entirely exclusion—the overwhelming emotional experience of one who is brought to see himself and his class—which happens to be the human race—as hopelessly tainted and deserving ostracism from any rational society. But let us reassure ourselves that this is not a drama of *Angst* and crisis in any Kierkegaardian sense. Suffering as he does a sudden conviction of guilt and displaying an extraordinary capacity for self-torture, Gulliver nevertheless remains a figure in a comedy. That is the paradox which so many readers and so many commentators have failed to grasp. *Gulliver's Travels* vexes, yet in more ways than one it is the merry work that Arbuthnot pronounced it. Here Swift's comic vision has found perfect expression.

VIII

FINAL PERIOD

When Swift returned to Dublin in September 1727 from what was to prove his last visit to England, he was nearing the end of his sixtieth year. The summer just past had had its excitements, for with the death of George I early in June Tories and discontented Whigs had enjoyed for a few weeks a vision of Walpole's fall and the creation of a new and broader Ministry. Swift, on familiar terms with both Bolingbroke and Pulteney, the latter the leader of those anti-Walpole Whigs who called themselves 'The Patriots', had confidently anticipated a change in the Ministry. And if those who had been excluded from all power since Queen Anne's death were to receive some representation, who knew what might follow? He had even allowed himself some faint hope of preferment in England—at long last!—and the possibility of a settlement there among his friends. But all these dreams had been dispelled as soon as Parliament had reassembled in the closing days of June, for the expected changes had not occurred, and Walpole and his Ministry proved as formidable as ever. Swift had never been one to feed on illusions. At home he was revered as the Patriot Dean and all the world was by this time reading *Gulliver's Travels*, but in his heart he felt that he was now an old man and that his greatest achievements lay behind him. He knew that he must live out his life here in Ireland. Stella's death in January 1728 confirmed as nothing else could this sense which had been growing steadily upon him that all now belonged to the past. Yet even in his decline his energy was astonishing, and for almost ten years—down into 1737, that is—he remained an active writer and a dominating public figure. The letters which he sent off to his friends in England were filled, to be sure, with constant references to his ill health and the deplorable conditions in Ireland, and as he wrote he often allowed himself to fall into that sensational language which came so naturally to him. Ireland was 'a mass of beggars, thieves, oppressors, fools, and knaves'. He was sick of the world, sick of age and disease, 'the last of which I am never wholly without.' He added, 'I live in a nation of slaves, who sell themselves for nothing.' And there were those unforgettable words about dying in Ireland in a rage, 'like a poisoned rat in a hole'. It is also obvious from all that has come down to us that he was an increasingly difficult person socially, his eccentricities of behaviour becoming more pronounced as the years passed. But the record of this final period as it lies before us in his extensive writings and in his varied activities as churchman and public-spirited Irishman throws a somewhat different light upon these latter years. True, there is nothing here on the creative side that is comparable to *Gulliver's Travels* or the *Drapier's Letters*, but the *Modest Proposal* is assuredly one of the most striking of his shorter prose works, and of the poems composed during his sixties a surprisingly large number stand among his more remarkable productions in verse. But it is the statesman that most impresses us—still the impassioned spokesman of Ireland's interest, and relentless as always in his realistic appraisals of what the nation was facing. If he was sensational in what he wrote it was only because he saw reason and common sense being disregarded so flagrantly. His despair—the despair of the complete realist—found its symbol in the macabre imagery of the *Modest Proposal*.

We may consider, first, the latter episodes in the career of the patriot Dean. The late 1720s go down in Ireland's history as years of great want and hardship. 'As to this country,' Swift wrote to Pope in 1729, 'there have been three terrible years' dearth of corn, and every place strewed

M

with beggars . . .' Whose fault? England's, primarily.
But the Irish themselves seemed bent on making a bad
matter worse:

> Imagine a nation the two thirds of whose revenues are spent out
> of it, and who are not permitted to trade with the other third, and
> where the pride of women will not suffer them to wear their own
> manufactures, even where they excel what come from abroad. This
> is the true state of Ireland in a very few words. These evils operate
> more every day, and the kingdom is absolutely undone, as I have
> been telling often in print these ten years past.

The list of his pamphlets and miscellaneous writings which
appeared at this time is a formidable one. It includes *A Short
View of the State of Ireland* (1728), a brief and impressive
summary of the situation in Ireland; *An Answer to a Paper,
Called 'A Memorial of the Poor Inhabitants, Tradesmen, and
Labourers of . . . Ireland'* (1728), a discussion of the evils
resulting from an overexpansion of the sheep-raising industry at the expense of agriculture; an essay on *The Hardships
of the Irish being deprived of their Silver, and decoyed into
America* (*The Intelligencer*, No. 19, 1728); *A Modest Proposal for Preventing the Children of Poor People from Being
a Burthen to their Parents or Country* (1729); and the *Answer
to the Craftsman* (1730), an ironic treatment of England's
policy of allowing foreign powers to recruit their armies in
Ireland.[1] Some years later, when it was proposed to lower
the gold standard in Ireland in order to bring about a better
adjustment of the entire currency, Swift threatened for a
while to lead, for a second time, a popular movement in
defiance of England's management of the currency. We

---

[1] In 1729 Swift wrote some six papers concerned with Ireland which for
one reason or another were not printed during his lifetime. Among these
were the *Letter to the Archbishop of Dublin Concerning the Weavers, Answer
to several Letters from unknown persons, An Answer to Several Letters sent
me from Unknown Hands,* and *A Proposal That all the ladies should appear
constantly in Irish Manufacture.* (See Herbert Davis, *Prose Works,* XII
[1954], Introduction.)

have, among other things, the *Speech Delivered by Dean Swift to the Assembly of Merchants . . . on the Lowering of Coin, April 24th, 1736*. In this instance Swift seems to have been quite wrong in his analysis; in any case, gold was lowered slightly in value by proclamation in 1737 with no disastrous consequences. One of the last of his Irish writings—it is dated 22 April 1737—is the *Proposal for Giving Badges to the Beggars in all the Parishes of Dublin*— evidence of how deeply-rooted in his thoughts was the problem of the indigent and disabled.

To these pamphlets must be added those called forth by incidents involving the Established Church and the position of the clergy. Three such incidents stand forth. The first concerned two bills which were introduced in the Irish Parliament in 1732. Known as the Bill of Residence and the Bill of Division, they had been sponsored by the Irish bishops and were designed, respectively, to compel newly-beneficed clergymen to build suitable houses when none were available, and to divide certain of the richer parishes. These were passed in the House of Lords, but the protests of the lower clergy were more effective in the House of Commons, where the matter ended with both bills being thrown out. Swift, siding with the lower clergy, threw his full weight into the fight against the bills, which he looked upon as devices on the part of the selfish bishops for 'enslaving and beggaring the clergy'. *On the Bill for the Clergy's Residing on their Livings* and *Considerations upon Two Bills*, written at this time,[1] are straightforward in every word; on

---

[1] *On the Bill for the Clergy's Residing on their Livings* was written near the end of January 1732, but apparently it did not appear at the time; the *Considerations upon Two Bills* is dated 24 Feb. 1731/2, a few days before the defeat of the bills, but seems to have been published a month after this, not in Ireland but in England. (See Louis Landa, *Swift and the Church of Ireland*, pp. 113-115.) But as Professor Davis points out in the *Prose Works*, XII, an abstract of certain of Swift's arguments in the *Considerations* appeared in the *Dublin Journal* on 26 February, the day the bills in question were rejected.

the other hand, the *Proposal for An Act of Parliament, To Pay off the Debt of the Nation, Without Taxing the Subject* contains an ironic counter-proposal to the bishops' bills. At about this same time the Dissenters were engaged in a campaign which had as its object the repeal of the Test, which had been imposed in Ireland in 1704 and had thus far withstood all assaults made upon it. This latest effort on the part of the Presbyterians and other Nonconformists to secure some modification of the laws directed against them met with complete failure at the end of 1733. Swift, greatly exercised, had contributed at least four pamphlets in defence of the Test: *Quaeries Wrote by Dr. J. Swift* (1732), *The Advantages Proposed by Repealing the Sacramental Test, Impartially Considered* (1732), *The Presbyterians' Plea of Merit* (1733), and *Reasons Humbly Offered . . . For Repealing the Sacramental Test* (1733), of which the last is cast in the ironic vein. Swift was saying nothing in any of these publications which he had not said repeatedly since he had first begun writing about Irish affairs: viz. if the Nonconformists demanded more than toleration it was because they desired political power, which they would use again, as they had in the past, to destroy the Church and tyrannize over all whose religious views differed from theirs. The third incident occurred in 1734 in connexion with a movement in the Irish Parliament to curtail certain of the clergy's tithes, and brought from Swift the protest contained in *Some Reasons Against the Bill for Settling the Tyth of Hemp, Flax, &c.*

The elderly Swift is to be judged as an Irish statesman in the broadest sense. On matters affecting the Church and on questions of religious policy his utterances were all in character and entirely in accord with his earlier statements, but though we may understand his position in both a logical and historical sense we are instinctively repelled by his restrictive attitude. As a writer on the secular problems of Ireland he produces on the modern reader an entirely different effect. Here he was at once realistic in his analyses

and practical in his recommendations, and though his socio-
logical views rested upon eighteenth-century assumptions
the earnestness and sincerity of his approach leave no doubt
of his genuinely charitable nature. To the manifold causes
of Ireland's general plight he returned time and again.
'I would be glad to know,' he wrote in the *Short View of
the State of Ireland*,

by what secret Method, it is, that we grow a rich and flourishing
People, without *Liberty, Trade, Manufactures, Inhabitants, Money*,
or *Privilege of Coining* . . . If we do flourish, it must be against
every Law of Nature and Reason; like the Thorn at *Glassenbury*,
that blossoms in the Midst of Winter.

England's economic policy in regard to Ireland and the
laws in restraint of Irish manufacture and commerce were
the main source of the nation's misery. Next, according to
Swift's reckoning, were the absentee landlords, who resided
out of the country—mostly in England—and drained away
a considerable share of the nation's wealth. In the sermon
on the *Causes of the Wretched Condition of Ireland* (precise
date of composition unknown, but probably after 1720),
after citing the 'intolerable Hardships' imposed by 'our
rigorous Neighbours', and the folly, vanity, and ingratitude
of the absentee landlords, he goes on to mention the pride
and vanity manifested by both sexes in their insistence upon
wearing clothing imported from abroad, the idleness and
sloth of the natives, who often 'chuse to beg or steal, rather
than support themselves with their own Labour', and the
cruelty, oppressiveness, and covetousness of the landlords,
'expecting that all who live under them should *make Bricks
without Straw*'. As the *Answer to a Paper Called 'A Memorial* . . .' shows, he was fully alive to the sequence of evils
which began in 'depopulation' (i.e. the uprooting of cottagers and farm labourers which occurred when previously
cultivated land was turned into pasturage). In consequence
of this shift from agriculture to sheep-raising the number
of itinerant beggars was increased, less food was grown at

home, and the wool market—suffering under restrictive legislation and Ireland's preference for imported fabrics—was
glutted, with disastrous consequences for the weavers of
Dublin. His proposals for positive action were entirely in
accord with such an analysis. The greatest hardship of all
—England's policy—and the greatest indignity—the cur-
tailment of liberty—would have to be borne, but not necessarily in stoical silence. The Drapier had shown how free
men might speak out so that even Whig ministers in London
would be forced to listen, and in 1726 Swift sought an
interview with Walpole in the hope, as he informed the
Earl of Peterborough, of representing the affairs of Ireland
in a true light, though he did not succeed in doing so.
Again, the absentee landlords could not be compelled to
live at home, but one might chastise them publicly for their
folly and ingratitude. Many of the economic hardships
could be lightened if Ireland could be persuaded to forgo
those luxuries which must be imported, to buy the goods
it manufactured in preference to others, and to use only
its own woollen products. Much could be done through
more sensible educational methods, particularly in the
charity-schools, which should prepare the children of poor
families for domestic service. There were definite improvements—in the way of better roads, better drainage of bogs,
better care of forest lands—which Parliament might encourage. But what is of much greater interest to us than the
specific proposals which he brought forward in tracts, sermons, and pamphlets is the spirit in which he approached
all these problems. Ireland was filled with visionary projectors who kept the public informed through an endless
series of *Letters* and *Proposals* of the latest schemes for
saving the nation. Swift's whole Irish campaign, from the
early 1720s down to the late '30s, was in a very real sense
an effort on the part of a great realist to make a nation look
facts in the face. So much could be achieved if people would
only dismiss all these dreams of easy remedies and quick

wealth and accept as a point of departure the actual conditions governing their lives! This was the burden of his *Letter to the Archbishop of Dublin, Concerning the Weavers*:

I am weary of so many abortive projects for the advancement of trade, of so many crude proposals in letters sent me from unknown hands, of so many contradictory speculations about raising or sinking the value of gold and silver . . .

If a private gentleman's income be sunk irretrievably for ever from a hundred pounds to fifty, and that he hath no other method to supply the deficiency, I desire to know, my Lord, whether such a person hath any other course to take than to sink half his expenses in every article of economy, to save himself from ruin and the gaol. . . . Therefore instead of dreams and projects for the advancing of trade, we have nothing left but to find out some expedient whereby we may reduce our expenses to our incomes.

In considering Swift's social theories we are to remember that the Drapier Dean was one of Dublin's most public-spirited citizens. In 1716 he helped to found a charity school in the Liberty of St. Patrick's. He erected an alms-house for 'ancient and orderly widows'. He served on the board of the Blue Coat School, officially the King's School, and of the Dublin Workhouse and Foundling Hospital. He was one of the subscribers to Dr. Steevens's Hospital and a trustee of that institution. And under the terms of his will he left a large part of his estate—some £7000 as it turned out—for the building and endowing of St. Patrick's Hospital for the insane. In addition, his private charities were large.[1] Swift never expounded the pleasures of bene-volence as English writers—many of them Anglican clergy-men—had been doing in increasing numbers since the last century. What purpose was to be served by dubious philo-sophizing when Christian precept and the social obligations incumbent on the more fortunate members of the com-munity made one's duty unmistakably clear?

[1] See Louis Landa, 'Jonathan Swift and Charity', *Journal of English ana Germanic Philology*, XLIV (1945), 337-50.

His theory of society, as we have previously seen from *Gulliver's Travels*, was an old-fashioned one which was, however, still entertained by many who felt called upon to discuss such topics as the social structure, class relationships, poverty, and organized charity. Swift's sermon *On Mutual Subjection* (of undetermined date) affords one of the clearest statements of his concept of the organic and hierarchical nature of society. Our particular stations in this graded scheme have been appointed 'to each of us by God Almighty, wherein we are obliged to act, as far as our Power reacheth, towards the Good of the whole Community.' Power, wealth, outward advantages are no marks of God's preference. Each man is bound by obligations to those above as well as those beneath him in the scale. Riches and poverty are to be looked upon merely as a trust, 'which God hath deposited with him, to be employed for the Use of his Brethren'. The two sermons entitled *On the Poor Man's Contentment* (date not fixed) and *Causes of the Wretched Condition of Ireland* (presumably after 1720) set forth his attitude towards the poor. There are, it seems, two kinds of poor: those who are miserable by reason of their own laziness and drunkenness; and the real, the deserving poor —'the honest, industrious Artificer, the meaner Sort of Tradesmen, and the labouring Man, who getteth his Bread by the Sweat of his Brow, in Town or Country, and who make the Bulk of Mankind among us'.[1] Swift was insistent that the distinction always be observed between the unworthy poor and those who had a rightful claim upon our charity. The latter were to be maintained by their own parish. In invoking parochial responsibility Swift was of course merely urging upon Ireland a set of principles which in England had been embodied in the Elizabethan poor laws. One of his favourite schemes is mentioned in the *Causes of the Wretched Condition of Ireland*:

[1] *On the Poor Man's Contentment.*

if every Parish would take a List of those begging Poor which properly belong to it, and compel each of them to wear a Badge, marked and numbered, so as to be seen and known by all they meet, and confine them to beg within the Limits of their own Parish, severely punishing them when they offend, and driving out all Interlopers from other Parishes, we could then make a Computation of their Numbers; and the Strolers from the Country being driven away, the Remainder would not be too many for the Charity of those who pass by, to maintain; neither would any Beggar, although confined to his own Parish, be hindered from receiving the Charity of the whole Town; because in this Case, those well-disposed Persons who walk the Streets, will give their Charity to such whom they think proper Objects, where-ever they meet them, provided they are found in their own Parishes, and wearing their Badges of Distinction.

It is this same scheme which is the subject of one of his last pamphlets, *A Proposal For Giving Badges to the Beggars in All the Parishes of Dublin* (1737). As has already been noted, Swift's views on education formed an important part of his positive social doctrine. In England the early decades of the century had been marked by a movement in support of charity-schools, and this had in turn called forth sharp opposition from those questioning the social expediency of this form of education. In Dublin, too, there had been much activity in behalf of charity-schools, and Swift had helped to found a new one, though he was in agreement with those who had been insisting that these institutions should not be allowed to train children for the trades. His discussion of these matters in the sermon last quoted from —*Causes of the Wretched Condition of Ireland*—shows how he applied his hierarchical principles to the educational system. Training for the trades might be permitted in the few charity-schools in Ireland enjoying private endowments, since these should be open only to children of 'decayed Citizens, and Freemen'; but there should be no training of this sort in the small parish schools, supported only by the 'casual good Will of charitable People'—such schools ought to confine themselves to preparing children for the meanest occupation in society, for otherwise

the poor honest Citizen who is just able to bring up his Child, and pay a small Sum of Money with him to a good Master, is wholly defeated, and the Bastard Issue, perhaps, of some Beggar, preferred before him.

As in so many other respects, Swift as social theorist reflects the ideas and temper of a period. If he was somewhat old-fashioned in clinging so tenaciously to the concept of the organic-hierarchical society, a concept which had already receded markedly before the new middle-class spirit and emergent utilitarianism, that was because of his essential clericalism, with its presuppositions concerning communal order.

The greatest of all the later writings on Ireland and his last prose masterpiece is the *Modest Proposal*. Though the straightforward tracts and pamphlets contain passage after passage marked by deep emotion as the misery in Ireland is described and the stupidity and perversity which are its causes are dwelt upon, the indirection of the *Modest Proposal* comes closer, one feels, to affording a full expression of his feelings. Here is ironic refraction with a vengeance and comedy in the full Swiftian sense. It is important that we take note of the full title: *A Modest Proposal For preventing the Children Of Poor People From being a Burthen to Their Parents or Country, And For making them Beneficial to the Publick.* The author—whether Dr. Swift, as the title-page indicates, or some other person is beside the point—is a public-spirited Irishman who has devoted many years to a diligent study of his country's needs. Like so many others of this stamp he is gravely concerned about the problem of population which confronts the nation. He is skilled in the new science of political arithmetic and can deal with humanity in the mass in the proper statistical fashion. He has already come forward with more than one project for the advancement of the general welfare, but he is now convinced that all his previous thoughts have been vain, idle, visionary. His present proposal, a method of making Ireland's prodigious number of children sound and useful members of the commonwealth, is not only wholly new but has something solid and real, and is besides 'of no expense and little trouble, full in our own power, and whereby we can incur no danger in *disobliging* ENGLAND'. This writer succeeds in convincing us, too, that his scheme has not originated in any motives of self-interest. But though the quickest way into the situation which Swift has created in this satire lies through the character supposed to be holding forth, the comic *mise en scène* is not to be accounted for solely in this manner. The irony embraces an entire period not only in Ireland's history but in social-economic speculation. The *Modest Proposal* is a parody of countless pamphlets dealing with population and poverty. It burlesques the manner and the methods of the early eighteenth-century political arithmeticians. Its purpose, however, is not to cast ridicule upon these pamphlets and these writers as such, nor is the satiric energy generated by this kind of parody and burlesque being turned against mercantilism as such. The doctrines of mercantilism and the specific principle thereof which held that people are the riches of a nation were all accepted by Swift. What the *Modest Proposal* does is to drive home the thing he had elsewhere insisted upon in vigorous but perfectly straightforward terms : in Ireland, conditions being what they are, human beings—the riches of a nation—are an insupportable burden, with at least five children in six lying 'a dead weight upon us, for want of employment'.[1] It is, of course, in the nature of comedy like this that far more should be involved than just the central themes and principles. Swift's humanity, his moral realism, and the intensity of his perceptions have all found expression in this short work which is so fully representative of his satiric genius.

[1] *Maxims Controlled in Ireland* (1729).

But it was through his verse as often as not that Swift impressed himself upon the public during this final period, and the impact of his personality is sometimes better gauged through the poems on politics and Irish affairs than through the prose we have just been speaking of. During all the stages of his career Swift was disposed to create certain almost symbolic figures which served as objects of an all-embracing contempt, appeared repeatedly in his satires, and bore the names of, and of course actually did refer to, people he knew and had come to despise. In the latter years most of the figures of this sort turn up in his occasional verse—in the libels and lampoons directed against Jonathan Smedley, Richard Tighe, Lord Allen, and Richard Bettesworth. These men were well-known in Dublin, and all of them had succeeded in arousing Swift's anger in one way or another, Smedley by personal insults, Tighe by informing against Sheridan, Lord Allen by taking exception to one of Swift's political poems, and Bettesworth, a member of the Irish Parliament, by supporting a bill affecting the clergy adversely. The poems in which Swift fell upon them are frequently coarse, always vigorous, and unforgivable if viewed in the light of present-day decorum. The earliest of these, *His Grace's Answer to Jonathan* (1724), had reference to Smedley; the latest, *On the Words Brother Protestants* (1733) and *The Yahoo's Overthrow* (1734), were concerned with Bettesworth; Lord Allen was the subject of the two parts of *Traulus* (both 1730), and Tighe appeared variously as Timothy and Dick in *Mad Mullinix and Timothy* (1728), *Tim and the Fables* (1728), and *Dick's Variety* (1728). Swift's language, if sometimes indecent, is wonderfully colloquial, and we are on occasion conscious of elements of a distinctly modern nature, as in *Mad Mullinix and Timothy*, which is cast as a dialogue between a crazy beggar and Timothy, Tighe's simulacrum. The satire begins as follows:

M. I own 'tis not my Bread and Butter,
But prithee *Tim*, why all this Clutter?
Why ever in these raging Fits,
Damning to Hell the *Jacobits*?
When, if you search the Kingdom round,
There's hardly twenty to be found;
No, not among the *Priests* and *Fryers*.
T. 'Twixt you and me G—Damn the Lyers.
M. The *Tories* are gone ev'ry Man over
To our Illustrious Home of *Hanover*.
From all their Conduct this is plain,
And then—*T.* G—Damn the Lyars again.

Walpole, the Irish bishops, the political state of England, and the Irish House of Commons were all subjects for treatment in the later verse. Two memorable poems of satiric commentary on English politics and English public figures are the *Epistle to a Lady* and *On Poetry: A Rhapsody*, both dating from 1733. In the former the poet, urged by the Lady to forgo his usual doggerel and sing her praise in the heroic style, answers that it is not in his nature to be grave and lofty; he is by birth the satirist, encountering vice with mirth:

Wicked Ministers of State
I can easier scorn than hate:
And I find it answers right:
Scorn torments them more than Spight.
All the Vices of a Court,
Do but serve to make me Sport.
Shou'd a Monkey wear a Crown,
Must I tremble at his Frown?
Could I not, thro' all his Ermin,
Spy the strutting chatt'ring *Vermin*?
Safely write a smart Lampoon,
To expose the brisk Baboon?
　　When my Muse officious ventures
On the Nation's Representers;
Teaching by what *Golden* Rules
Into Knaves they turn their Fools:

> How the Helm is rul'd by [Walpole]
> At whose Oars, like Slaves, they all pull:
> Let the Vessel split on Shelves,
> With the Freight enrich themselves:
> Safe within my little Wherry,
> All their Madness makes me merry:
> Like the Waterman of *Thames*,
> I row by, and call them Names.
> Like the ever-laughing Sage,
> In a Jest I spend my Rage:
> (Tho' it must be understood,
> I would hang them if I cou'd:)
> If I can but fill my Nitch,
> I attempt no higher Pitch.
> . . . .

On Poetry: A Rhapsody is full of good things. There are the well-known lines describing the natural state of war among the creatures—

> a Flea
> Hath smaller Fleas that on him prey,
> And these have smaller Fleas to bite 'em,
> And so proceed *ad infinitum*—

and applying this to the commonwealth of letters, where

> ev'ry Poet in his Kind,
> Is bit by him that comes behind . . .

The entire passage in question is a triumphant imitation of Samuel Butler not only in the attitude of contempt towards mean poetry and paltry poets but in rhythmic movement, rhyme, and figurative language that is at once witty, grotesque, and logical. And there is the poet's tribute to the Augustus of the modern world, George II:

> Fair *Britain* is thy Monarch blest,
> Where Virtues bear the strictest Test;
> Whom never *Faction* cou'd bespatter,
> Nor *Minister*, nor *Poet* flatter.
> What Justice in rewarding Merit?
> What Magnanimity of Spirit?

What Lineaments divine we trace
Thro' all the Features of his Face;
Tho' Peace with Olive bind his Hands,
Confest the conqu'ring Hero stands.

In the couplets which ensue the other members of the royal family are similarly complimented, and Walpole, 'Of Wit and Learning chief Protector', is described in terms of fitting panegyric. If praise of kings and ministers is ordinarily a prostitution of the Muse, in England it is impossible for the poets to 'err on Flatt'ry's Side'. Such satire may be regarded as part of the great anti-Whig drive which to a certain degree had been mapped out at Twickenham by Swift, Gay, and Pope in the summers of 1726 and 1727. *Gulliver's Travels*, with its political allegory, had been followed up by the *Beggar's Opera*, packed with insults directed at Walpole and his party, while the present poem was to be matched by Pope in due time, notably in his epistle *To Augustus*, with its satiric address to George II.

The last great diatribe occasioned by Irish affairs was *The Legion Club*, coming at the close of Swift's active career. In 1736 the Irish House of Commons gave its support to the landowners as against the clergy in the matter of certain tithes then under dispute, and the Dean's anger found expression in this famous invective. Here is Ireland's Parliament House, here the demoniacs who inhabit it, their name Legion like that of the unclean spirit:

Could I from the Building's Top
Hear the rattling Thunder drop,
While the Devil upon the Roof,
If the Devil be Thunder Proof,
Should with Poker fiery-red
Crack the Stones, and melt the Lead;
Drive them down on every Scull,
While the Den of Thieves is full,
Quite destroy that Harpies Nest,
How might then our Isle be blest?

Since the 1690s Swift had been engaged in putting words together, and he could not stop now. When he was not writing on Irish issues and personalities he turned to more general themes. Quite a false impression of the final period of activity would be conveyed were something not said of the writing purely literary in character, writing very considerable in extent and sometimes of the highest quality.

In 1728 Swift and Sheridan undertook to put out a weekly paper called *The Intelligencer*. Their first number appeared on 11 May, but after nineteen issues the enterprise was allowed to die (though an additional number, containing one of Swift's verse satires on Dean Smedley, was added later). Swift contributed both verse and prose to the *Intelligencer*, a most interesting essay on the *Beggar's Opera* constituting the third number. Gay's ballad opera had been put on in Dublin not long after its first London performance on 29 January 1728, and though the Dean had never been a notable defender of the theatre and modern plays he lost no time in recording his enthusiastic approval of his friend's work, which fitted so well into the anti-Whig campaign discussed at Twickenham. Swift's essay is of added interest in that he took this opportunity to enter upon a discussion of humour—a discussion, alas, altogether too brief and not always so clearly pointed as might be wished. Previously, in the poem *To Mr. Delany* (1718), he had distinguished between wit, humour, and raillery. The latter he defined as 'That Irony which turns to Praise.' As for wit and humour :

> by Wit is onely meant
> Applying what we first Invent :
> What Humour is, not all the Tribe
> Of Logick-mongers can describe ;
> Here, onely Nature acts her Part,
> Unhelpt by Practice, Books, or Art.
> For Wit and Humor differ quite,
> That gives Surprise, and this Delight :

Humor is odd, grotesque, and wild,
Onely by Affectation spoild,
Tis never by Invention got,
Men have it when they know it not.

In the paper appearing in the *Intelligencer* he takes Temple's essay *Of Poetry* as a point of departure. In discussing modern drama Temple had given it as his belief that humour on the stage and the word *humour* were both peculiar to the English. Humour, he had written, 'is but a Picture of particular Life, as Comedy is of general', and had gone on to show how the English dramatist had only to depict those 'originals', those humorous men, which his country produced in excess of all other lands:

... where the People are generally poor, and forced to hard Labour, their Actions and Lives are all of a Piece ... We [in England, on the other hand,] are not only more unlike one another, than any Nation I know, but we are more unlike our selves too, at several times, and owe to our very Air, some ill Qualities as well as many good ...

Swift agrees that the word is peculiar to our language but will not accept Temple's view that the thing is confined to the English nation. Humour is 'in some manner fixed to the very nature of man', the taste for it is purely natural, and the talent for it is by no means confined to men of wit and learning, for the meanest of people often possess it without being aware that they do. Though contemned by the critics as low humour or low comedy, it is, nevertheless, the 'best ingredient toward that kind of satire ... which instead of lashing, laughs men out of their follies, and vices, and is the character which gives Horace the preference to Juvenal.' Swift's general drift is clear enough, but he would seem to have had certain distinctions in mind which his phrasing rather blurs. For one thing, humour in the old medical sense seems to have been identified—some peculiar disposition which makes a man what Temple termed an 'original'. Allied to this but at the level of creative imagination would be that talent which leads us to speak of one who possesses it as a man of humour, a writer of humour. There is the humour that we acknowledge in anecdote, poem, play; and lastly, the taste for humour, the enjoyment of a certain kind of conversation or art. How, it is natural to speculate, would Swift have applied all this to himself and his work? The eccentric characters he had created in the *Tale of a Tub* and elsewhere were probably thought of as humorous in the first of these senses—they were 'originals'; he himself would be a humorist—humorous writer, humorous satirist—by virtue of a natural gift for conceiving situations and fictional characters of a surprising and original order.

Early in the autumn of 1731 Swift wrote to Gay that he had retired to the country for the public good, having two 'great works' in hand, one 'to reduce the whole politeness, wit, humour, and style of England into a short system for the use of all persons of quality', the other to be a Whole Duty of Servants—complement, that is, of the famous book of piety, *The Whole Duty of Man*—from steward down through all the ranks to scullion and pantry-boy. The first was *Polite Conversation*, or more fully *A Complete Collection of General and Ingenious Conversation, According to the Most Polite Mode and Method Now used At Court, and in the Best Companies of England*. It was published in 1738, and its reception in Dublin was such that it was even produced on the stage—the only dramatic presentation of a work of Swift's that one is aware of. The sheer length of the piece, consisting of three dialogues, is the outward sign of the amazing energy with which the verbal play has been sustained. In a linguistic comedy such as we have in Swift's early poem about Mrs. Frances Harris there is likewise no end of verbal play, but it has all been made to seem an essential part of Mrs. Harris's personality. In *Polite Conversation*, on the other hand, the words are more important than the characters—indeed, it is the words that are using such creatures as have here been assembled. There is a diabolic quality in this comedy of *clichés*, for the verve and enthusiasm which go into recording the endless stream of expressions are answered by complete emptiness on the part of the characters. The second work mentioned in the letter to Gay was the *Directions to Servants*, published in 1745 shortly after Swift's death. It is often amusing, but it is scarcely in the same class with *Polite Conversation*.

It was in verse, however, that the elderly Swift expressed himself most readily, and the poems of the late 1720s and early '30s are in themselves enough to prove that his talents suffered no sudden decline. This later poetry is marked, furthermore, by a much greater diversity of theme and manner of treatment than the casual reader is likely to notice. Such poems as *Helter Skelter* (1731) and *The Place of the Damn'd* (1731) show what effects Swift was able to achieve when he gave himself over, without any reservations, to rhythmic and word patterns. *The Grand Question debated* (1729) is reminiscent of at least the spirit of *Mrs. Harris's Petition*, though the lady's waiting woman who holds forth in the later poem is a remarkable creature who can conjure up resplendent social scenes with a vividness that would do credit to a poet. There are poems of social satire like *The Furniture of a Woman's Mind* (1727) and *The Journal of a Modern Lady* (1729), and those completely ruthless studies in discontinuity, *The Lady's Dressing Room* (1730), *A Beautiful Young Nymph* (1731), *Strephon and Chloe* (1731), and *Cassinus and Peter* (1731). One of the strangest of all his poems, imaginatively powerful and leading up to a singularly effective ending where the discovery and reversal of traditional drama are matched by a sudden descent into colloquialism, is *Death and Daphne* (1730), addressed to his friend Lady Acheson, mistress of Market Hill, where Swift spent many months as a guest. According to this poem Death has come to town in search of a wife; he transforms himself into a fashionable beau, and in the course of his rounds meets the lady and becomes enamoured of her. The lady, who feels sure that she has only to exercise a little wit to win another admirer, talks glowingly of the lower world, the fops, beaux, toasts, and gallants one could meet there, and how pleasant it would be to ride along the banks of the Styx in one's coach:

> What Pride a Female Heart enflames!
> How endless are Ambition's Aims!
> Cease haughty Nymph; the Fates decree
> *Death* must not be a Spouse for thee:
> For, when by chance the meagre Shade
> Upon thy Hand his Finger laid;
> Thy Hand as dry and cold as Lead,
> His matrimonial Spirit fled;
> He felt about his Heart a Damp,
> That quite extinguish't *Cupid's* Lamp:
> Away the frighted Spectre scuds,
> And leaves my Lady in the Suds.

The greatest of his poems of self-characterization, *Verses on the Death of Dr. Swift*, likewise belongs to this period, having been composed in 1731. His satire is here justified and defended in the traditional terms: he aimed to correct vice, he directed his attacks at general classes, not individuals, he never ridiculed natural deformities:

> "He spar'd a Hump or crooked Nose,
> "Whose Owners set not up for Beaux.
> "True genuine Dulness mov'd his Pity,
> "Unless it offer'd to be witty . . .

Memorable are the lines of this famous poem sketching the social scene and describing the conversations that take place in various groups as news is brought of his death:

> My female Friends, whose tender Hearts
> Have better learn'd to act their Parts.

Receive the News in *doleful Dumps*,
"The Dean is dead, *(and what is Trumps?)*
"Then Lord have Mercy on his Soul.
"(Ladies I'll venture for the *Vole*.)
. . . .

But the poem that is perhaps most characteristic of his later years is the *Day of Judgement* (1731). The Jove who is speaking in it is, let it be noted, only an imagined figure and his language is suspiciously full of Swift's own colloquialisms. What we have, by design, is an old man's vision, grim and at the same time comic:

With A Whirl of Thought oppress'd,
I sink from Reverie to Rest.
An horrid Vision seiz'd my Head,
I saw the Graves give up their Dead.
Jove, arm'd with Terrors, burst the Skies,
And Thunder roars, and Light'ning flies!
Amaz'd, confus'd, its Fate unknown,
The World stands trembling at his Throne.
While each pale Sinner hangs his Head,
Jove, nodding, shook the Heav'ns, and said,
"Offending Race of Human Kind,
By Nature, Reason, Learning, blind;
You who thro' Frailty step'd aside,
And you who never fell—*thro' Pride*;
You who in different Sects have shamm'd,
And come to see each other damn'd;
(So some Folks told you, but they knew
No more of Jove's Designs than you)
The World's mad Business now is o'er,
And I resent these Pranks no more.
I to such Blockheads set my Wit!
I damn such Fools!—Go, go, you're bit".

IX

EPILOGUE: 'I SAW A WOMAN FLAYED'

MUCH of the time Swift was a thoroughly representative figure, reflecting his own age in manifold ways. Even in those instances where he seemed to differ from his contemporaries his position was never a genuinely eccentric one and can usually be accounted for in terms of principles and presuppositions to be found somewhere within the period. Thus his theory of the ordered society was one which in the modern era had been voiced since the days of the Tudors, and by no group more persistently than the Anglican clergy. Though it fell with an increasingly clerical accent upon a generation that was turning more and more to social individualism and finding its image in the works of Locke, it was still a perfectly familiar concept and remained so throughout the eighteenth century, as we are reminded whenever we read Samuel Johnson. His doctrine of rational liberty went directly back to the great political controversies culminating in the Revolution of 1688. His ethical and moral views were not those which eventually came to prevail in the Enlightenment; nevertheless the kind of rigorism which he embodied from first to last was not an individualistic or temperamental thing but a well-defined attitude towards human nature, an approach to human conduct, having a definite history in thought and letters. In countless ways, intellectually and in general temper, he stood in the tradition of post-Restoration Anglicanism. He was nowhere more completely eighteenth-century than in his doctrine of common sense, with its concept of the normal man—completely sane, completely representative—and its rejection of wayward enthusiasm and too-eager speculation.

In his early pamphlets on Church and State, in the work

he did for the Tory Ministry, in all his publications concerned with Ireland Swift was the public writer. It is unfortunate, though of course inevitable, that this entire side of
his career, being closely engaged with the events of a bygone
day, should stand in need of so much historical commentary
before revealing its essential features. He had set forth his
basic principles regarding State and Church in his first
pamphlets, and he never at any time departed from the
political concepts defined there nor from his early theory
concerning the Church and its relationship to the secular
power. He began as a Whig and ended as a Tory, he gave
himself up to strident partisanship, he was ungenerous to
his enemies, he was often sensational beyond need, but he
was always fighting to preserve what he thought of as the
freedom of free men. Freedom in the practical sense was
freedom from political tyranny, but it bore a larger meaning when seen as that discipline which both the individual
and society could achieve by exercising reason, self-control,
and common sense. Apart from the beliefs he defined and
the causes he espoused he is distinguished by his magnificent command of the rhetoric of public discussion and
controversy. The range of subjects taken up in the pamphlets and tracts is a wide one but scarcely suggests the very
great variety in his style and his approach. Each occasion
meant a particular audience and required that this be
addressed in a manner that would produce exactly the right
effect. Swift was always a rhetorician—even in his satires,
even in his most sensational moments—but never more
completely so than in his public writings, which from a
stylistic point of view are unsurpassed in their kind among
English letters.

It is as satiric artist that Swift's individuality is most
striking, but here too it is necessary to see him in his age
if we are not to misinterpret the spirit in which he worked
and the effects he achieved. It is really a question of defining for ourselves the situation of the literary artist in the

Enlightenment. The nineteenth century made the mistake of trying to interpret eighteenth-century letters in terms that were still essentially those of Romantic art and experience. The Romantic myth which established itself throughout Europe in the decades following upon the French Revolution gave to the self a new importance and looked to individual and highly personal experience for its themes. The Enlightenment simply did not think and feel and express itself in this way. If it had a myth, it was that of the normal man and normal, representative experience. Its literary forms were established and well-differentiated types —the epic, the pastoral poem, etc.—governed by accepted principles of composition essentially rhetorical. So far from remaining untouched by this spirit prevailing in the world of letters Swift was in his own way fully responsive to it. When he wrote on public matters, he showed how well he understood the meaning of decorum through use of a style exactly suitable to the occasion at hand. In his poetry he was almost always guided by his sense of genre, imitating Horace, working with the language and rhythm of Samuel Butler, and again parodying the matter and superficial manner of the pastoral. Nor did he, as a satirist, break with this general tradition. He saw satire as having its proper function within both the social and the literary scheme. Furthermore, for the chastisement of folly and the depiction of the ridiculous there were appropriate devices of style in the way of theme, imagery, and an order of language.

But in considering the literary artistry of this pre-Romantic age we must not allow ourselves to stress this aspect of decorum, formalism, and rhetoric to the exclusion of the truly imaginative elements always present in the greater writers and most assuredly so in Swift. We use *imagination* in the broad sense that it commonly bears in modern criticism, remembering that Swift's own period scarcely understood this application of the term. They spoke rather of *genius, talent, invention,* indicating by *imagination* the image-making faculty or, when the implication of creativeness crept in, the wild fancy of the enthusiast. But their art was more than skilled craftsmanship. Swift's satires gave expression to a view of man and of human life which, though not precisely ours, is no longer subject to the kind of misinterpretation that found its way into so much nineteenth-century criticism. The comic view did not awake aspirations, it afforded no visions of progress, no glimpse of new regions of experience. It was completely mature in recognizing the limitations of all our moral and intellectual resources. It is perhaps least admirable in its insensitivity to what Milton and others had already conceived of as the progressive revelation of truth through time and experience. But we must take it for what it was, and value it because of its admirable hatred of all the forms of delusion and false aspiration. Freedom from self-delusion did not bring happiness as the fool and the knave conceived it, but until we attained that kind of freedom we could not be free in any other sense. Civilization—the life of reason, of decency—began in seeing ourselves and the circumstances of human life as they really are. 'Last week I saw a Woman flayed, and you will hardly believe how much it altered her Person for the worse.' Only Swift could have put it that way.

SELECT BIBLIOGRAPHY

I. COLLECTED EDITIONS

The Prose Works of Jonathan Swift. Ed. Temple Scott. London, 1897-1908. 12 vols. (Bohn's Standard Library.)

The Correspondence of Jonathan Swift. Ed. F. Elrington Ball. London, 1910-1914. 6 vols.

The Poems of Jonathan Swift. Ed. Sir Harold Williams. Oxford, 1937. 3 vols.

The Prose Works of Jonathan Swift. Ed. Herbert Davis. Oxford, 1937-   (in progress). Of the 14 vols. projected, the following had appeared by the close of 1953: I, II, III, VI, VII, VIII, IX, X, XI. (The Shakespeare Head Edition.)

II. OTHER EDITIONS

A Tale of a Tub, To which is added The Battle of the Books and the Mechanical Operation of the Spirit. Ed. A. C. Guthkelch and D. Nichol Smith. Oxford, 1920.

Vanessa and Her Correspondence with Jonathan Swift. Ed. A. M. Freeman. London, 1921.

The Drapier's Letters to the People of Ireland. Ed. Herbert Davis. Oxford, 1935.

The Letters of Jonathan Swift to Charles Ford. Ed. D. Nichol Smith. Oxford, 1935.

Journal to Stella. Ed. Sir Harold Williams. Oxford, 1948. 2 vols.

III. BOOKS OF SELECTIONS FROM SWIFT'S WRITINGS

Satires and Personal Writings by Jonathan Swift. Ed. W. A. Eddy. London and New York, 1932.

Swift: Gulliver's Travels and Selected Writings in Prose and Verse. Ed. John Hayward. London and New York, 1934.

The Portable Swift. Ed. Carl Van Doren. New York, 1948. (The Viking Portable Library.)

A Selection of Poems by Jonathan Swift. Ed. John Heath-Stubbs. London, 1948. (Crown Classics.)

Selected Prose Works of Jonathan Swift. Ed. John Hayward. London and New York, 1949.

Swift on his Age: Selected Prose and Verse. Ed. C. J. Horne. London and New York, 1953. (Life, Literature, and Thought Library.)

IV. BOOKS ON SWIFT, BIOGRAPHICAL AND CRITICAL

(in chronological order)

Forster, John. *The Life of Jonathan Swift*, vol. I [no more published]. London, 1875.

Craik, Henry. *The Life of Jonathan Swift.* London, 1882. 2nd ed., London, 1894. 2 vols.

Stephen, Leslie. *Swift.* London, 1882. (English Men of Letters.)

Whibley, Charles. *Jonathan Swift.* Cambridge, 1917. (Leslie Stephen lecture, delivered 26 May 1917.)

Pons, Émile. *Swift: les années de jeunesse et le 'Conte du tonneau'.* Strasbourg and London, 1925.

Williams, Sir Harold. *Dean Swift's Library*. Cambridge, 1932.

Quintana, Ricardo. *The Mind and Art of Jonathan Swift*. London and New York, 1936. Reprinted with additional bibliographical material, 1953.

Jackson, Robert Wyse. *Jonathan Swift, Dean and Pastor*. London, 1939.

Ross, John F. *Swift and Defoe: A Study in Relationship*. Berkeley and Los Angeles, California, 1941.

Davis, Herbert. *Stella: A Gentlewoman of the Eighteenth Century*. New York, 1942.

Case, Arthur E. *Four Essays on 'Gulliver's Travels'*. Princeton, New Jersey, 1945.

Davis, Herbert. *The Satires of Jonathan Swift*. New York, 1947.

Johnson, Maurice. *The Sin of Wit: Jonathan Swift As a Poet*. Syracuse, New York, 1950.

Starkman, Miriam Kosh. *Swift's Satire on Learning in 'A Tale of a Tub'*. Princeton, New Jersey, 1950.

Williams, Sir Harold. *The Text of 'Gulliver's Travels'*. Cambridge, 1952.

Bullitt, John M. *Jonathan Swift and the Anatomy of Satire*. Cambridge, Massachusetts, 1953.

Price, Martin. *Swift's Rhetorical Art: A Study in Structure and Meaning*. New Haven, Connecticut, 1953.

Ewald, William B., Jr. *The Masks of Swift*. Oxford; and Cambridge, Massachusetts, 1954.

Landa, Louis A. *Swift and the Church of Ireland*. Oxford, 1954.

Murry, John Middleton. *Jonathan Swift, A Critical Biography*. London, 1954.

INDEX

References are to persons and to the works of Swift. References to the Preface are omitted.